Advance Praise

Whether we live in trauma and turmoil, boredom and loneliness, or overall making excuses, there are often any number of life's debacles that women may encounter. We may not always know how (or, take the time) to follow through in listening to our inner voice, understand and expand our horizons in discovering more about what we are meant to be and do, and/or know how to enhance our own relationships. That is when the book *Heal Your Trauma, Heal Your Marriage* piqued my interest. Having personally dealt with health-related conditions over the years, I was inspired by the work that Dr. Cheri McDonald did in her amazing work with clients while promoting how to re-discover our "true selves."

– Cheryl J.

I feel that even though it seems geared toward marriage, I was benefitting a lot from what the book said. I am a single person, but I have relationships with other people in my life that I know I will benefit in how to feel and conduct my reactions to certain situations that come my way. This is such an informative book and makes it simple to understand and relate to.

– Caren B.

Hail to Dr. Cheri McDonald for authoring a beautiful book on how to break the bonds of trauma and wholly embrace relationships and their full potential! A very healing read!

– Kristin S.

Heal Your Trauma, Heal Your Marriage takes a topic that can seem scary and emotionally difficult, and makes it easily digestible and relatable to the masses. This book explores complex PTSD in a way where anyone in any kind of relationship can benefit and learn from, in a kind, open manner.

– Emily S.

Many people in life go through big traumatic events, and many more (I would say everyone) goes through little daily traumas that impact your sense of who you are, your value to yourself and others, and your sense of safety and responsibility. These internalized perceptions of yourself have a huge impact on your interpersonal relationships including your marriage. Many times people are reacting to their spouses based on faulty beliefs they developed from their past traumatic experiences. Dr. Cheri offers great insight and actual tools to help Individuals and couples heal from the trauma as they can have healthy relationships that they want. Heal the trauma, heal your marriage.

– Whitney H.

This book is amazing. It gives so much hope for what can be transformed in one's life. I felt so connected to the steps to take to achieve my best self, and accept and let go of past traumas. I think everyone can find something relatable in this book, which can help transform and redirect one's life.

– Lexi H.

Heal Your Trauma, Heal Your Marriage

Heal YOUR TRAUMA, Heal YOUR MARRIAGE

7 STEPS TO ROOT, REBOUND, AND RISE

DR. CHERI MCDONALD

NEW YORK

LONDON • NASHVILLE • MELBOURNE • VANCOUVER

Heal Your Trauma, Heal Your Marriage

7 Steps to Root, Rebound, and Rise

© 2020 Dr. Cheri McDonald

Published in New York, New York, by Morgan James Publishing in partnership with Difference Press. Morgan James is a trademark of Morgan James, LLC. www.MorganJamesPublishing.com

ISBN 9781642797466 paperback
ISBN 9781642797473 eBook
ISBN 9781642797480 audiobook
Library of Congress Control Number: 2019948160

Cover Design by:
Megan Dillon
megan@creativeninjadesigns.com

Interior Design by:
Christopher Kirk
www.GFSstudio.com

Morgan James is a proud partner of Habitat for Humanity Peninsula and Greater Williamsburg. Partners in building since 2006.

Get involved today! Visit
MorganJamesPublishing.com/giving-back

*I dedicate my work and book to all those survivors
who taught me to never quit, to put one foot
in front of the other until the miracle happens,
and to make my dreams come true.*

Table of Contents

Foreword

As a student of mine, I have known Dr Cheri for the past 3 years, and I am excited to share what she is about and how come you will want to read what she shares. Dr. Cheri's expertise manifests in her teachings from the heart, where she masterfully guides you to the discovery of your Inner Healer for life-altering happiness and sense of purpose. She has now expanded on this in *Heal Your Trauma, Heal Your Marriage: 7 Steps to Root, Rebound and Rise,* where she demonstrates how we can all rise above and beyond our trials and challenges to *be* and live our potential joyfully.

As a 5th Dimension Quantum Healer, this is exactly my story, as my journey has included lifetime of defying experiences, in which, I knew I was bound for more. I, Dr. Cheri, and now you can too, have chosen to embrace our self-awakening paths. When the call came to me to embrace my purpose, and I made the choice to take it, it included stepping into the power of love, live love and teach love. My call is to be the Energy Healer I am, and to get there, I can say I did walk through the 7 steps of Dr Cheri's *Triangle of Mastery*.

Although, we come from different orientations, lands and paths as Healers, we are one in the name of love. As an expert, Dr. Cheri's insightful steps, as presented within this book, masterfully walk you through the "hard", shedding the pseudo-self-identities from the past traumas, to discovering your divinity and mission to embrace and, as you do so, finding truth and happiness along the way. Dr. Cheri's experience of working with thousands of individuals and families, combined with over thirty years as a Healer, has helped her create the steps that changes lives. As a mentor, Dr. Cheri lives her purpose through her evolvement as a psychotherapist, hypnotherapist, energy healer and life mastery coach. Dr. Cheri is sought out for these services, as well as, an author, professional speaker and consultant. I believe that if you follow her steps and seek her out, you too, can break out from the bondage of all your past trauma, *be* free and then, make your dreams come true.

Zarathustra
Founder of 5th Dimensional
Quantum Healing & Awareness

Chapter One:

Trauma Bound and Broken Hearted

"To be sure, man's search for meaning may arouse inner tension rather than inner equilibrium. However, precisely such tension is an indispensable prerequisite of mental health. There is nothing in the world, I venture to say, that would so effectively help one to survive even the worst conditions as the knowledge that there is a meaning in one's life. There is much wisdom in the words of Nietzsche: "He who has a why to live for can bear almost any how."
— Viktor Emil Frankl, Man's Search for Meaning

L ife with complex trauma can be misery, and to imply that it is anything less would minimize the impact Post Traumatic Stress Disorder's (PTSD) destructive nature has ushered in for so many. I liken it to an entangled web that has no beginning nor ending; hence, once you realize you are in it, you also realize your greatest fear: There's no escape and being held hostage by your past forever. Fortunately, this is not reality. The mere fact that you are attracted to my book is confirmation that you do have at least an inkling of awareness that there is hope in untethering yourself from its grip. Most of us accept the concept that life has its peaks and valleys; some days are better than others. Most everyone strives to make each day a good one in our earthly experiences of love, laughter, and living happily ever after. What we aren't prepared for is when our world is hit with one bad day after another. We aren't prepared for the valleys filled with pain and suffering to never end with no peak in sight.

This monstrous mass has no discernment of who it hits. You are not alone in waking up to find yourself enveloped in a dark cloud of trauma which has blinded you from seeing the deterioration of your life until its crumbled completely… or so it feels. Complex trauma is experienced by everyone to one degree or another, and many have so little knowledge on how to manage their lives when its destructive path has crossed their threshold. Now, it's found its way to your doorstep. This book addresses the PTSD fallout and how to *rise* above and beyond to become whole again. It addresses the avenues of healing for you and then your *marriage* in every aspect of your life. I address the committed union as it applies to the integrity we give to every type of relationship in life, and how every aspect of your life is directly impacted by PTSD. So, if you are in a life phase that traditional marriage is not the relationship interplay with the ramifications of your distress, the *The Triangle of Mastery's 7 Steps to Root, Rebound and Rise* apply to all transitions of healing and rising. Your relationship works as a mirror in which your spouse reflects your misery and self-sabotaging patterns that are taking you and your marriage down. The challenge is to save not only yourself but your marriage as well. As you *re-awaken* and recognize you do not have to *be* your PTSD and lose your dream-come-true marriage, the first step to re-claiming your life is to stop and do something different. By starting where you are at, you can begin now to *rejuvenate* from your loss and *real-I-ze* the need to show up by *renewing* the love that defines you. By doing so, you will *revive* the healing power of love within your marriage as our intuitive promptings serve you, call you to act and *resurrect* your broken heart to *rise* to your Ideal Self. As you do this, you can become one in heart with your spouse again and heal your marriage.

Now, it is my finding that everyone has experienced trauma, just in different degrees. It is usually one that is above and beyond that is a *slam, bam, thank you, ma'am,* crippling you to the point of reading this book. My clientele is drawn to me when an event impacts their life directly or indirectly and they are hit with an a-ha! *awakening, realizing* they do not want to feel their pain any longer and looking to *rise* out of the rubble. These events can be anything from within and without the relationship such as, discovered secrets of deceit, loss of a loved one, financial ruin; or tragedy that comes across their path like, victims of terrorism, violent crimes, disease, and natural disasters.

This is a new era with the commitment to show up, the time to reflect and step back to the beginning of you. At first, this may sound counterintuitive, as today's story is screaming, "When will this pain stop? How could my spouse be saying he is done, then tell me I am too difficult, and he is tired of competing with my PTSD?" How do you stop and think about your kickstart into this life when today is crumbling all around you, when you are wrestling through an avalanche of emotions that make you feel like damaged goods and unable to see that there is a purpose to live for anymore?

The answer is… you just do. As it is, you have nothing more imperative than crawling out of this carnage and reclaiming your life. Once you are *risen*, then you will have the capacity to heal your marriage. And now you have found the place where you will be led to the how, what, when, why, where *to love and beyond* as your intuition now is calling out to you. You may be wondering as to how this happened? Yes, you are quite aware of your pain and suffering, yet your husband has been your rock. What happened to break him? When did he truly begin to breakdown and decide this merry-go-round ride has ended for him and he wanted off? Why and why now? And where are you to go now? Lost in the dizziness of the never-ending torment, left to do it alone seems unbearable. Yet, when all seems lost, there still is hope *and* the whisperings from deep within will show you the way out from the dark clouds, out of strangulation of the web, out of the valley, and into the light once again.

As human beings, unlike the rest of the animal kingdom, we are gifted with the ability to see ourselves. We are observers when we remember to be. It is your observing eye that has brought you to this point. As I believe there is no such thing as a coincidence and everything has its purpose, this step of learning how to navigate out of this despair is your purpose.

You may ask how come the journey from pain and suffering is so difficult, especially when the destination you are seeking is to be joyous and healing. If I told you that that this is simply perspective and attitude is everything, you may want to throw this book across the room, so I won't. I will share what I was taught that has been helpful with my clients to muster up the stamina and internal fortitude to invest in themselves. I was told once that comfort is the number one addiction in our society. The familiar is comfortable; the unknown is not. As a result, it is not uncommon to resist stepping away from what we know. However, since change is the only true constant in life, lack of change leads to stagnation. This explains P.T. Barnum's statement in the 2017 movie *The Greatest Showman* that "comfort is the enemy of progress." Seeking out this book indicates you are uncomfortable, and now you are in motion to progress. Each movement brings change and it is change that can give you hope.

I know just reading this does not create motivation for true effort toward change. Resistance to leave the comforts of familiarity is strong and a common thread in how society functions. Yet now you are at the edge of your cliff and following the pack will lead you right off the edge to your demise.

Much of the reason for this is pure ignorance of not understanding how. Sometimes there's fear that change is too hard and painful when in actuality change creates momentum that's freeing and enlightening as it directs you to the starting line to the path to the race that will take you to your desired destination.

It took me decades to hear and then listen to the whisperings from within and then even longer to following the impressions of my inner healer, my *Ideal Self*. As I learned and continue to learn, I have discovered the treasure of wisdom and arrived at the place where I am empowered to heal the wounds of my remaining injuries and clear the scar tissue formed from experiences and failed efforts to heal the fractures and complexities of life. Without checking in and conversing with your inner compass, you are at the mercy of falling to the whims of the PTSD complexities despite the attempts to forget, deny, and rush ahead so that life plans are not disrupted and life milestones are checked off as planned.

The truth of the matter is we are here on earth to learn from our experiences, and this includes the painful and frightening ones. I like to think the phrase "there is a silver lining behind every cloud" is a truth not just a cliché, and behind every trauma there is an opposite to gain. Many women find themselves in a divorce for a wide range of reasons. However, when PTSD tears a couple from one another, its dark cloud sneakily blankets the relationship, blocking the light from shining on them, leaving them to wither away into nothing over time. With no light, the couple loses sight of one another, *awakened* to find they are estranged and unable to see past the PTSD impact. The most common questions asked are, "Why are these things happening to me? How can we ever recover from these experiences, memories of pain and destruction?"

You may also be asking yourself if you do come out from under the rubble, "How do you ever return to normal again?" No doubt your self-image is hurt as this *real-I-zation* comes when you are at your lowest and feel things could not get worse. In her book *Hope for the Flowers*, author Trina Paulus offers a great analogy of how a caterpillar attempts to make it to the sky to fly by joining the ranks of others to create a caterpillar pillar, only to find the journey to be filled with dismay and disillusionment and then to fall to the ground and hit bottom. Like the caterpillar, you too may have felt your life has been a delusion. After plummeting from the top of the caterpillar mountain and belly flopping, hitting the ground, and knocking out the last bit of breath you have, your hard fight for what you thought was the right was a free fall of terror. The way toward your happily ever after butterfly flight is met with the *real-I-zation* that you were without your wings to carry you forward. This realization tends to open a floodgate of emotions as shock and denial of the loss you are facing dissipate. Now that you are grounded, you are faced with embracing feelings of anger, despair, and pain that took you down with its gravity pull, offering you this opportunity to address and free yourself once and for all from its burdensome weight. What are you to do with this loss of innocence? Knowledge is power, and this *is* knowledge. And with knowledge comes responsibility, the responsibility of crawling out from under the carnage of nightmares and to *re-awaken*.

This self-awareness I speak of tends to show up in the wee hours of the night. It is during *REM* (rapid eye movement) sleep that you vet out the negativities of the day. It's not unlike the cocooning of the caterpillar's metamorphous into a butterfly. Unfortunately, rarely are we able to get through our unfinished business of the previous day before morning breaks; hence, the dawn breaks before our wings spread, and we are left to carry any remaining angst forward into the next day. Over time, the unfinished business accumulates, and the hopes of flying dissipate as the cocooning process is not completed and the progress is grounded. This becomes the emotional baggage that you bear on your shoulders and carry in your heart known as unresolved pain and anguish. Over time, this buildup of grief chains you to the past and prohibits you from *rooting* in the present, *rebounding* with resilience, and rising to your freedom. Instead, you are left in the yesterdays being lost, unable to learn how to fly forward into the present. This state creates a fight of futility; without *rooting* to complete the cocooning your wings cannot *rebound,* you cannot *rise*. This leaves you stuck where you are at and with only what you know and left to feel there is nowhere to go. You are left in the past, yet not really as the past no longer exists. You are living a story of pain created by your inability to process out the remaining angst, memories, and emotions that detour your ability to be whole and eventually, lead to your collapse. In this collapsed state where you are peeling your face off the ground from diving off your mountain of rubble, all feelings of love and joy are seemingly lost to you. Broken, you look around and find yourself alone on the ground, too weak to get up yet nowhere to go, you're left to cover yourself with your broken wings to for whatever protection they can offer. However, the comfort is scant; your fears and unresolved grief are fed with shame that is a paralyzing and germinating field for nurturing the pseudo-self. The pseudo-self feeds on the toxicity of shame; this poisonous persona is what you have left to share with your world. Now, can you imagine what you project which may explain what you receive in return? No wonder your marriage is collapsing as your fear emanates a toxicity that neither one of you can seemingly *rise* out from under. Left with this *stuckedness* and unable to complete your cocooning, you become vulnerable to disturbances that are stalking you through the days and haunt you through the nights filled with daymares and nightmares. You may find yourself lying down at night and, before your head hits the pillow, breaking down in tears – like Pavlov's dog! – only to wake up to the tear-soaked pillow from the early morning, memories of the cycle of trauma you have come to find yourself trapped in. This evolves into patterns of *stuckedness* that manifests, as overwhelming feelings of fear and regret throw you into a cycle of self-loathing and learned helplessness.

Why does this occur? I have learned from my clients that they realize they have been duped by their PTSD, and now faced with discord and threats they crumble under what they now recognize as the armor of shame, prohibiting them from showing up with the intimate vulnerability a marriage requires. Although you want to claim it's come out of nowhere, your inner whisperings remind you otherwise. The coping mechanisms of yesterday projected into the present are discovered to be barriers and the enemy of intimacy. Knowledge is power, and by allowing your ears to hear this quiet voice from your inner healer, you are now free to recognize the enemy for what it is. Fear that you are a day late and a dollar short is natural for the both of you, yet this, too, is another lie. At first, left to your own devices, you may seek control as you engage in your patterns of reactivity and thinking in all or nothing terms only. This is again the PTSD mechanisms at work kicking you into the world of entrapment of the black and white paradigm of seeing.

Black and white thinking evolves as a coping mechanism in living with the ramifications of PTSD, and it's a faulty one. The overwhelming feelings of trauma flood your system, which can become unbearable. This avalanche of emotion is a self-preservation mechanism, in which your mind will usually manage only seven pieces of information to filter one at time so that decision-making and choices can be made.

At the same time, it filters out the same number to maintain steadiness and clear thinking. However, as trauma hits, your filtering system may become compromised, resulting in your inability to filter and you become flooded with all or nothing of information and feelings. The natural reaction is for your brain to then switch to what I refer to as the *all-or-nothing* switch or the *black-and-white* thinking pattern. This processing *feast-or-famine* throws you into becoming a glutton of demanding over indulgence or isolating from all the true love and joy you desire. You are either all-in or all-out, which, takes you out of the present. You are escaping into the fantasized past or the learned helplessness of pining for an unreachable future (without being in the *now*), you are unable to process new and present-day information. Rather, you are left to compensate and obtain a sense of control by whittling down the information you receive to one piece and then letting go of only one piece, which manifests as "either/or" and sometimes "my way or no way". For all intents and purposes, you are seeking to get your footing and feeling steady, safe, and whole in the world of unresolved chaos. Yet, without the *rooting* that begins with cocooning from the inside out, you are quickly tossed to and from by the winding cycle of your trauma.

This *black-and-white* thinking can give you a sense of control and stability in keeping the PTSD manageable for you well enough. If, you were an island unto yourself. Unfortunately, it is detrimental to your relationship. In the marriage, this manifests into everything being all good or all bad. You are all good or all bad, and your spouse is also all good or all bad. This cycle of love/hate, down/up, good/bad has taken your marriage down.

This *black-and-white* perspective has no tolerance for good enough and has impacted your ability to find comfort and security with your spouse, preventing a deeper bond based on acceptance. An example of this thinking process is you can quickly change from thinking your spouse is perfect to feeling the opposite. This yo-yo swinging creates a shaky foundation, rapidly eroding intimacy, and trust. The ability to see yourself and your spouse as normal and fallible human beings is lost in the paradigm of either all good or all bad.

Randy is a woman who prides herself in loving her husband; she loves to share their magical story of how they met and found love at first sight. As she shares this aspect of her fairy tale life, one's heart experiences over-flowing feelings of joy and awe of the love story they share. Then without taking a breath, Randy switches to her stories of nightmarish episodes of contention, betrayal, and heartache she harbors toward her prince charming, who is now anything but charming. She is unable to address the continuum of human vulnerabilities that come in the cycles of life. This projection of all-good-or-all-bad, creates a gulf of presence that allows for processing growth and hope for present-day intimacy. As a result, the pseudo-self throws her marriage into a storm of chaos and lostness unknowingly, pulling their union into the trauma cycle of never-ending turmoil. Now Randy and her spouse are living their life, held hostage by the past and guarded by their pseudo-selves shielded in their rusty armor. Intimacy is gone, love lost replaced with emptiness and confusion in which healing and re-igniting the passion of their union seems only a dream far, far away.

As you can see now, the dilemma remaining is your attachment to the safety you know in the confines of the *black-and-white* thinking, which is strong. The rewards of defining yourself as the wounded one can feel too hard to give up. In the book *The Knight in Rusty Armor*, Robert Forest's infamous knight fights off fire-breathing dragons to rescue damsels in distress. Lost in his enthusiasm of his adventure and success, he fails to take time to change out of his armor. Its rusted hinges imprison him, and he must go off to face his own past to get his freedom back. It is now that he realizes he lost sight of himself and the princess he married. She no longer knew him to be the hero she wedded and would only take him back if his rusted armor was off. This analogy brings to light how sly the past is in creeping up in our lives and impeding our connection to one another. It may be more common that well-intended endeavors are used by the pseudo-self to create pain and distance. The armor was the protector; but when worn as a barrier, it becomes a major block to any intimate connection at home.

Stopping and *rooting* to observe and then *rebound* from the trappings of the slippery slope allows you to *rise* above and see with the eye of the true self, which I have coined the Ideal Self. It is here that perspective from above can be recaptured and action in the now can be taken.

These feelings are strong and real and do require a firm decision to fight to break out of the rusted armor and trust the inner whisperings which brought you to this point. The bondage represented by the rusty armor can be defined by the word *woundology*. In 1988, author and medical intuitive Carolyn Myss invented this term to support her theory that some people don't heal because they have created an identity out of their woundedness. Based on Carolyn Myss speaking of *woundology*, this marriage feeds the ego, likened to the knight in rusty armor, by giving them attention, titles, and *wins* in life they don't want to give up. You may find yourself struggling to hold on to what is familiar and the battle of the internal *tug-a-war* of *it's too much* and *it's too hard* to imagine the possibility of healing. Yet this then leaves you with being buried alive under the avalanche of self-betrayal brainwashing from the PTSD. And your ability to get a grip slips out of your hands. This bondage of *woundology* is the home of our pseudo-self, locking out your Ideal Self.

Prior to gaining a grasp on your PTSD, your sense of self is calcified by the rusting from the ego. Although you have felt connected to your spouse, his experience has been the opposite as he has been unable to see the *you* behind the armor, and here is where the heartache lies.

The trauma brain fails to recognize the actual interconnectedness with reality. It only recognizes the physical realm or finite sphere and sees everything as separate. The two hemispheres experience what I refer to as a fracturing. To explain, take the Humpty-Dumpty analogy (since this is the very analogy my clients have used to educate me on how they feel and experience their life); you have a whole brain to work with, then trauma hits you like a two-by-four to the back of a head. You go tumbling down. You hit the ground hard, and you are cracked and fractured into many pieces. Although you are all there, any sense of wholeness is gone, and you cannot discern which end is up. In an attempt to get your bearings, you grab all the fractured pieces and hold them tight to your body in hopes of not missing a part. This becomes all you can do, frozen in time, lost on what to do, no sense of grounding nor ability to *rise*. Broken, the communication frequencies go static, and all connections are hindered. Now the gulf is created, and this fracturing is the new norm. This fractured brain is handicapped by the hit of the trauma, and each fragmented piece is left to frantically seek a connection. In turn, your focus turns to managing the mis-firings of the fractured pieces, and you fall into a pattern of fearful pushing and pulling at your relationship. Since you are thrown into a cycle, there is no end in sight, circling around and around the merry-go-round and seeking the light at the end of the tunnel of the fantasized past and future. As you continue on this treadmill, everything operates like a machine, yet only within the confines of the merry-go-round ride. Hence, your point of view is off, the frequency interference keeps you blinded from the relationship, and you lose sight of you and the duality in life and love.

Your loss of awareness of your spouse's experience and paradigm creates the splintered connection of pain and chaos, in which you no longer aligned to one another. Decisions are reactive as all sense of conscious living is overshadowed by the armor that has rusted while fighting to preserve each broken part. In turn, these fragments within your brain engender a belief that you have no free will over what is happening; you create a perspective that nothing can change and God is doing this to you. Such belief reflects a calcified ego in which internal confusion dictates every breathing hour and you remain tormented with an insatiable appetite of lostness due to lack of understanding truth. Your focus, then, fixates on seeking comfort for the pseudo-self.

In truth, this pseudo-ego has robbed you of your true intelligence, true care, true courage, and true will, as they are insignificant to the ego. The ego's goal is to hold you hostage to the urgency and to entrap you in concerns for your physical survival and daily operations in life.

Maslow's Hierarchy of motivation speaks of this. He outlines the five needs we evolve through motivating us toward personal evolution:

1. Physiological – food and shelter
2. Safety – security
3. Belonging and love, intimacy, and friendships
4. Esteem – feelings of accomplishment
5. Self-actualization – achieving full potential

As you will see in further discussion in Chapter Four, trauma stalls the evolution through these needs for fulfilment, complete healing, and becoming love.

This is *stuckedness,* a failure to flow and *rise* through each level that creates deficiency of our needs met. The PTSD's black and white paradigm blocks the realization that deprivation is temporary and can even create a greater drive to move up the hierarchy. This block turns to an insatiable appetite of staying stuck in the first two levels, as the ceiling creating a trickery of perception and denial of growth and expansion as the mechanism of endurance. An *all-or-none* phenomenon replaces the natural ebb and flow of personal growth and relationship building.

Understanding your personal trauma cycle (the animal of PTSD) and where you start in the tumultuous journey you have endured is the first step in combatting your fears and moving forward from the *now*. The natural appetite for growth is sabotaged and replaced with *stuckedness.* Now that you are aware of the potential dangers you may have created for yourself, you can change the tide.

Every person is capable and organically has the desire to move up the hierarchy toward a level of self-actualization. Progress may be disrupted by your trauma's interference. As human beings we have more tenacity than we recognize. You can begin your climb today one step at a time.

The PTSD's deceit has blinded you to your consciousness and spirituality, and it significance rises to the surface when absent from your relationship. The lie heard from your trauma voice may be, "What is happening to other people is happening to them and not me; all I need to worry about is my own comfort and my own survival, and that is what my husband wants as well." This has trapped you in an illusion, believing in fantasy and buying into lies about who you and he really are.

You can come to know yourself, gaining a concept of your true nature and embracing your Ideal Self. In turn, being able to do the same for your spouse, equipped to make your cocoon for the metamorphosis phase to begin. Here you will come to know who you are at a higher level of self-knowledge, to understand self-knowledge of our psychology and physiology, how energy works throughout the body, and how to take care of the vessel that hosts our consciousness. This is a marvelous, magnificent, and miraculous wonder you are embarking on.

I can only imagine the strength, courage, and faith this is taking as you reflect on your story and the challenge of taking on your pseudo-self who, in it's calcified stated, cannot envision the true freedom you seek. Shedding the rusted armor demands rising above the influence of the agenda serving your egoic will. You have caught the vision of your calcified ego's drive to getting what it wants and its destructiveness if not curtailed. As the pseudo-self is without care of what love and joy have to offer, it creates a pattern of destruction. In turn, it has no need to bond with another, for it feeds on perpetuating its self-serving agenda, its need to avoid change and personal growth, and its hold onto the victim archetype. In the end, as you can now see, the pseudo-self with its calcified ego is unable to comprehend the torture you suffer and the cost of losing sight of your desired dreams coming true. By recognizing your story, you can now see that you've been perpetuating the opposite dynamic of what you professed you wanted to manifest.

And you may still be asking how, what, why, when, and where. There are many levels to PTSD, and this is the complexity of it all. The most recent focus on trauma is the developmental trauma that comes from simply growing up, as I shared earlier, starting with the cutting of the umbilical cord. Yet there are also theories that stories handed down through the multi-generations are stored in our DNA and passed down through the cells of our bodies. As intelligence of energy, how can we say, "This isn't so?" And if so, are the complexities of the PTSD web unfathomable to expect to ever comprehend?

On face value, the answer may be an unequitable *yes*, yet as we explore a bit more deeply it can be a *no*.

Yes, we ponder the possibilities and their impact on the psyche. And no, if we stick to the basics and work to get to know your Ideal Self, develop the capacity to love from the inside out, and then make room for your marriage.

The knowledge that you carry predispositions for some of the chaos you experience and create brings the ball back to your court. Remember knowledge is power; now that you have the ball in your hands, you can choose how to play the game, what to play, why play the game at all, when to show up, and where to begin.

If you hold on to the ball and don't share, you are caught in the trappings of the PTSD cycle and become victim to a life without intimacy. One common symptom of trauma is becoming emotionally numb and disconnected from those who are closest to you. Chronic PTSD causes loss of interest in all things once enjoyable and can lead to downward spiral of disengaging, leaving you to live out the trauma and flashbacks day and night. The waves of emotion and physical sensations from the mimicking intensity of the PTSD soon replaces the connection to the marriage. If left and not addressed, PTSD can progress to literally changing brain structures, resulting in functioning differently, as author Debbie Hampton addresses in her book *Beat Depression and Anxiety by Changing Your Brain*.

In turn, your spouse is left alone in a marriage of "intimacy anorexia" (Doug Weiss) – in other words, they're starved of love. This truth can be uncomfortable, harsh, and ugly. Yet, now that you have come out of the dark shadows of the victim archetype where you are no longer wedged in the chaos, you can notice the truth and witness it not need be so horrifying, depressing, or negative but actually uplifting and empowering. The truth, in its entire splendor, beauty, and horror, positive and negative, is there for the self-betterment of your pseudo-self. Like the instructions given in *Karate Kid*, "wax on, wax off". As you align to your Ideal Self, the two selves (your pseudo-self and Ideal Self) can meld together to get a grip on your life, improve understanding, and come into harmony with your inner healer and conscious expression.

The truth is what you are after now, and truth is what is the most important to reach anything good, prosperous, beneficial, and uplifting. This may not be the part you want to accept as the truth, as it can be uncomfortable to hear, can feel hurtful, harsh, unpleasant, etc., and can cause you to feel insulted, offended, guilty, or shameful. This is necessary for your positive development towards alignment with your Ideal Self, with what is right, good, and *true!* These emotions are your compass in life giving you a signal that you need to pay attention to its warning of something not right. And something is not right in your world now.

Alignment with truth requires truth! The person speaking truth is speaking truth, not lies. The insult, offense, shame, guilt, etc. that you feel is generated by your trauma and pseudo-self. In your ego's refusal to align with truth, you have aligned with falsity, lies, deceptions, and illusions.

Attaining self-knowledge, self-realization, and self-actualization is having come online and connecting with your higher levels of consciousness. It is breaking out from the clouds of deception of the PTSD that keeps you in a *stuckedness* state of mind and consciousness. Now that you know and realize, *you know more that you know you know*, you can take action to break through the mindset nurtured by the trauma cycle. You can now capture the butterfly's perspective from the skies above, free from the trappings of the rusty armored. This world view offers endless possibilities, in which, you can see beyond the black and white thinking that comes with trauma. Together, we can define your roadmap for personal evolution and marital bliss.

Your task is to understand how things fit together so that you come to a level of consciousness where you can re-ignite the passion in your marriage. As you come to understand your truth, you will come into being with greater degrees of alignment with your spouse and make your dream come true. Viktor E. Frankl's *Man's Search for Meaning* puts all this in a nutshell for you to see where you are going and the desired destination to guarantee a happily ever after:

"Love is the only way to grasp another human being in the innermost core of his personality. No one can become fully aware of the very essence of another human being unless he loves him. By his love, he is enabled to see the essential traits and features in the beloved person; and even more, he sees that which is potential in him, which is not yet actualized but yet ought to be actualized. Furthermore, by his love, the loving person enables the beloved person to actualize these potentialities. By making him aware of what he can be and of what he should become, he makes these potentialities come true."

Chapter Two:

My Story

*"If only our eyes saw souls instead
of bodies. How different ideals
of beauty would be."*
— Unknown

My introduction to tragedy arrived just before I turned five when our home was struck by German Measles, a windfall to me and my brother from preschool. Unknowingly, we exposed my five-month pregnant mother, resulting in my baby sister being exposed and inflicted with Cerebral Palsy. As my eyes fell on this hand-sized purple-dotted infant encompassed by this disease, I felt my little bubble of paradise burst – an innocence lost in the moment as I witnessed the imminent price this invading parasite caused to this smallest of creatures, my baby sister. The inflictions impaired her physical development as she was deaf, crippled with deformities and a compromised immune system. Paralyzed and scared with this *real-I-zation,* my life was turned upside down, newly defined in a moment, and my world was never to be the same.

The purity age five gifted me offered no shield for me from ownership of the blame for bringing this contagion to my baby sister. Then her loving nature, which seemed to wrap itself around me as an eternal circle of never-ending compassion and acceptance, emphasized the shame of robbing her of the potential life of wellness.

Survivor's remorse buried me alive. I shut down, not knowing how to show up as the light around me dimmed to a blackness that blinded me from any reflection in life that offered reprieve of my broken heartedness over something I could not fix. My life was spinning, and I felt no control as I landed into this new paradigm of hopelessness, loss, and dismay which, quickly redefined who I was and who I was to become – and continues to make me into the person I am today.

Reflecting on the new world I was spun into, the reality I had now was shattered forever. I had accepted my shattered world as I embraced this as part of the plan God had for me, yet the gnawing sadness remained, blocking my ability to settle into my own skin and show up for life.

This sadness became a constant companion isolating me from my peers and activities that were offered to others. Through my growing years and with each milestone in life, I would be haunted by the increasing contrasted life paths of myself and my sister, riddled with trauma residual feelings of guilt and self-blame.

One day, I woke up knowing I had to do something to divorce myself from the chronic sadness and getting a grip on my own PTSD. Someone once shared with me that if we could take the Diagnostic and Statistical Manual of Mental Disorders V that mental health professionals use for assessing for treating clients, if whittled down to one diagnosis, it would be unresolved grief. This conversation has stuck with me as it seemed to be exactly what I had witnessed, yet it also rang deep with my being as the defining element in my story.

I was *re-awakened* with a new awareness that the *me* who I began to *be* in the first five years of life was nestled in the arms of my inner healer. She was my Ideal Self waiting for me to wake from the unending grief I was swallowed up in until now. Now I knew I could dig myself out from under the rubble of despair and be reunited with the joy of innocence and abundance of love within me as its soothing energy healed my broken heart. Being *awake* and ready to go was one thing; it was quite another matter to know how to pole-vault forward. Then the impression which sprung me forward to taking the first step of *rejuvenation* spoke in my ears as I heard a messenger instruct me to learn hypnosis. By taking the directive as an inspirational answer to my dilemma, my journey began.

I came to the *real-I-zation* that this was the start of my life story, in which I took center stage as the main actor. It began with my personal experience with hypnotherapy. I attended a group regression session as part of a training. My hypnotic journey took me to a realm where the veil is very thin, and I experienced a confirmation of what I *knew* yet only solidified at this time.

I had a life-altering experience which I refer to a pre-earth vision. This vision came to me during a hypnotic session which involved me and my sister Lori before we were born. Lori refused to allow me to come to earth with the handicap instead of her. I argued profusely, but she was calm and said she had accepted this calling, or mission in life, and this was her choice. As the vision ended, it was most clear that Lori's handicap is a part of her purpose on this earth. Tragedies and tribulations are all part of a bigger plan. This plan, although unseen much of the time, is where the core of purpose in life is to be found, the chosen path discovered, and the key for true change resides.

This pre-earth vision opened my eyes to the landscape already laid out for me. All I had to do was be willing to see the unseen, hear the unheard, and know I know more than I know I know! I woke up to a sense of knowing there is much to *do* in my life. As I experienced this new *real-I-zation*, my mind expanded, and I couldn't spend another moment sleepwalking through life. I knew I had to take action now, yet this *real-I-zation* still was only a concept.

My vision of myself during the life dialogue with my baby sister reminded me that I am *always,* and I am created with purpose. This immediately led to writing my book, *Whisperings from Within – Creating and Achieving Your Ideal Self.* I felt *commanded* to do what I ask of my clients, to get to know myself for who I am and walk alongside them through their path to do the same. This became the beginning of the ICAN (*I Create and Achieve Now*) mantra, which *renewed* my spirit and provided a blueprint to launch from.

This blueprint worked as a reminder that I was on the search for understanding of just *how* to manifest God's will for me and to complete the yin-yang dynamic of sisterhood envisioned. Yet, the journey to write was not about the book; rather, it was about the experience in and of itself. I had to encounter the world of my clients while I confronted the obstacles that blinded me as I entered foreign lands where I could expand my talents and abilities. My vision opened to new horizons in a twinkling of an eye as the veil to our multidimensional playground presented itself. This dual awareness started to show up with signs and wonders in every interaction and experience in my life. I had learned the power of my creative imagination and the language of my inner healer through the whispering from within. I was grounded in my stand and *rooted* into the blueprint of my evolution, allowing my master healer to *rebound* and *rise* to the occasion. Knowing what I was being called to was one thing, yet *real-I-zing* I was lost prior to the vision was another thing. I was starting out with no sense of how to show up in this world. I was an empty shell and had no connection with my Ideal Self. This *real-I-zation* now commanded me to embrace life, *rise* above my past trauma, and show up as my highest and best Self. I lived on the fantasies of a fairy tale life I created in my quiet times through my growing years and pretended to be what I perceived others needed me to be. As a result – I'm sure you have guessed already – I mastered co-dependency skills that gave the illusion that I was "ok" and had acquired the secrets of life.

My trauma manifested in my emotional development. As a child, I observed the overwhelming responsibility for my parents, and attempting to make room for them to be present for my sister, I stepped aside. I focused on being as good as I could to not take up energy and space. The by-product was I shut down my connection with my emotions and lost sight of myself. I created my own armor that rusted and barricaded me from knowing the miracle I was and celebrating the miracle of others. I became invisible in plain sight, the last thing I wanted, yet I succumbed to the saboteur within me. I could not grasp the concept of purpose in this divine positioning of where I landed in this world. Prior to my *re-awakening*, the challenge to show up was overwhelming and confusing. I was most aware of the pain and suffering I perceived as my parents' world and sought to meet them where they're at in my mind. I, unconsciously, took on the persona of the orphaned child to fall in place in the family system as my restitution to the tragedy that befell us. My tribal purpose was no longer the same, and I independently detached and sought direction to rectify matters and to have something to bring to my family circle as an initiation back into the tribe. Little did I understand that this was my creation, my powerful influence that persuaded all to follow my lead. The consequence of this compulsion to feed and react to the guilt and state of lostness created negative self-judgment and stifled my maturity. Since my reaction was to retreat versus act out, I was able to home in on the other aspects of myself, which, encouraged me to resurface and search out other surrogates to lead to where God intended me to present myself in this sphere of existence.

Yet this did not come without great struggle; much of my search was done from the spectator perspective as I purposefully kept life at an arm's distance. The greatest barrier to overcome was breaking through the armor of my persona and mantra… *All is well, and I'm here to save you.* I had mastered the ability to show up in a specular performance of the female version of the white knight in shining armor and save the day for many while shielding my own vulnerability from being exposed.

As time went on, I struggled to move through knowing and into action. My life cycled back into a lull period. I *re-awakened* and re-*real-I-zed* I remained buried alive in my armor and was suffocating. Despite, my life's evolution into a beautiful and blessed picture of fortune, including a marriage for twenty-five years, mothering four healthy and brilliant children, and playing in a busy and thriving psychotherapy private practice, I had yet to metamorphize into my Ideal Self.

I knew how to create a picture of perfection, a Pollyanna world, and remain in my self-made grave where no demands to intimately show up would occur. Despite my pursuit of education and exploration of talents, my sense of lostness remained. This lostness triggered a of sense of failure and feeling of not being good enough. My revelation filled my being with bliss, which escaped me now as I failed to continue my *rise* to becoming my Ideal Self. Rather, my evolution became stagnant, and now I was consumed with feelings of being dis-eased from the inside out, despite the knowing my family and I were afflicted with from the outside-in. This dis-ease is residual of the affliction of survivor's remorse; unresolved guilt and sense of responsibility lingered and now seemed bigger than life itself. The overwhelming feelings buried me alive in the grave of despair.

I soon became aware that life searching had led me to parts of my purpose yet not the core. The more I created in my life, the more the emptiness filled my soul. The full life I created on the outside fooled me and everyone around me. I presented a life that was full and complete, yet I was anything but complete. As this *real-I-zation* surfaced, I experienced my own *aha* moment that brought clarity and meaning to the picture. Everything was happening in God's time. I needed this *lull* period to give me the opportunity to reflect, *rejuvenate*, and reacquaint myself with *being* me. All the while, I was being led down the yellow brick road toward self-discovery to get me back home. God never stopped paving the way; He even carried me when needed to keep me on track.

I reflected on all the teachers and mentors that worked with me during this time with the courage and gumption to hold a mirror up for me to see who they saw beneath the armor. The vibrational energies of what I heard resonated within me, and the intimacy of my empathic nature began to *re-awaken* from the depths of my soul. I welcomed the embarkings of my own union and opened myself to the newfound love and joy germinating in our bonds of matrimony. This *rejuvenation* process, flooded with the *real-I-zations* accumulated along the way, came together to bring the messages forward to begin my story.

I shed my armor quite easily at this point, as the process of breaking through the metal construct had begun years ago; I only had the last welding grip of my own hands to release it to fall off from me. As I claimed my empathic nature, my intimacy anorexia no longer barricaded me from life. This reframe freed me and gave me a *renewed* sense of life as God created me to live. I was not needed as a wounded or orphaned creature; I was made to be magical, to do marvelous work and bring wonder to all by showing up.

Now free from my armor, I was no longer hostage to my past. Instead, I have a grip on my PTSD and am at liberty to choose how I want to use it to better connect and love others. I quickly learned how *real-I-zation* and doing and then being are three different animals. It was time to create my blueprint and align with my inner healer. It was the season to cocoon. The Heart Math Institute woke me to the power of the heart and how it is the center of *renewal* for life, longevity and actualization. I attended a seminar in 2004 where they taught a simple technique of expressing appreciation toward achieving a way to a deep connection via my heart. They placed our forefinger in a receptor which recorded our heart rhythms. We then were instructed to imagine speaking from our hearts, not from our heads and out our mouths. We were to allow the heart to express appreciation for whatever came to us over and over. From the heart, we were to express "I appreciate…" until we witnessed the rhythm on the monitor change from rapid up and down lines across the screen to a soft rolling line going up then down. This procedure took us to our inner healer's rhythm, where the body reportedly enters its natural *renewal* and regenerative mode. Upon following their meditative method, I broke through to my intimacy capacities and opened the channels to my intuition and inspiration. This revolution of science resonated and cleared the fog of confusion in knowing how to manifest the blueprint presented to me from within. As I claimed the power of my heart and communed with the loving essence shared by my inner healer, I was able to pick up from where I left off with the five-year-old orphan to begin the magical and *renewing* journey together.

This cocoon process required me to become a builder of my home as I worked to *revive* my Ideal Self and come out of the shadows and into the light. This preparatory work provided the strength and stamina to *be* personally vulnerable as I *revived* my light with brilliance of the new day dawn. Now present and in plain sight, I was ready to *restore* my strength from the inside out. As someone who spent their childhood living in the shadows of others, this was a great endeavor.

As I *real-I-zed* I had no know-how, I searched out mentors that would get me there. Marshall, an entrepreneur coach, taught me to live boldly, act courageously, and *be* strong. To do so, he introduced me to the "wax on; wax off" paradigm to open my horizon and my eyes to what belief systems were working for me and/or handicapping me.

Then Jack, my writing coach, taught me the value of my voice and how to begin to show up. I learned it is ok to start where I am at, as this is exactly the right place for me while I embrace my power of choice to *resurrect* my Ideal Self. The inner cry to *resurrect* led me to another mentor; Zarathrustra, 5th Dimensional Quantum Healer, who invited me to his training for energy healers in Are, Sweden. We were taught how to open our third eye Chakra and see our energy fields for self-healing and then to teach others to do the same. We see what the inner healer sees, to come to know what we truly know and be who we are meant to be.

It was the early morning prana yoga classes that proved to be my cocooning time. Through taking the time, making the space, and showing up for breath of life, I allowed myself to commune with my inner healer, integrate all the insights I gained from my mentors, and architect the blueprint of my life. Now in my resurrected state, I *revived* my core values from my *roots* to work as stakes in the ground and launch forward.

Synchronically, as I befriended the core values to launch this next phase, I came across an ancestor of mine whom I had not known of; her name is Carolyn Crow Swallow. She was born in the 1820's in Essex, England, was married, and the mother of eight children. She is my great, great paternal grandmother. It was said she was a petite, intelligent, and devout woman. Known for her gift of tongues and prophecy, she was nicknamed as a prophetess for her gift of offering insight to missionaries whom she welcomed into home for food and shelter. Despite her ordinary life and small stature, she showed up with her empathic outreach unique to her. She knew more than she knew she knew, and openly and freely shared it. Upon reading her story, I felt an immediate kinship and a knowing that she was my mentor, a ministering angel, and a frequency channel for my communication with the other side of the veil.

Carolyn's story came to me at a time I could understand the mission I was forming with my cocooning. Her role model was the invitation to discovering my intuitive abilities and become a witness to how they showed up as I observed my own evolution. The more I acknowledged my gifts, the more they surfaced. My clair-cognizance demanded that I shine the light forward and was able to see, speak, and sense my clients needed me to successfully guide them through their journeys.

My paradigm had shifted, and I had strengthened my wings enough to break through my cocoon. As my wings spread and I flew to heights beyond my imagination, I quickly learned the secret to the final lap for success. I learned that our *resurrection* comes from going through the passage *To Love... & Beyond*, which is action from within and outside of the therapy room. Within the confines of my personal life adventures, I showed up to stand tall within my *Triangle of Mastery* and walk the *7 Steps to Root, Rebound, and Rise* that fit my world as I successfully integrated with my inner healer and opened the way toward transforming into my Ideal Self. Because each of us are unique, we need individualized direction and tools to get us where we are destined. This has taken me on a continued search and integration that I now offer all who would come my way.

As for me and my story, I learned of purpose and miracles. Through this awareness I now know this wisdom comes from the spirit. In turn, this spiritual awakening is manifested through an earthly body of ageless-ness; from the mouth of babes, to the last breath from the most aged on earth, and everything in between. I learned by embracing the power of knowing that miracles show themselves and all is possible. Coming from a place of emptiness, in which, I felt like I was haunted by an imaginary demon, I fractured. The dis-ease that entered our family home, blinded me from my path and bonded me to the hopelessness that comes from finite thinking and kept my limited perceptive. As I have opened my ears, eyes and mind to the infinite gift of understanding, I've arrived at a place where I assist others and, this opportunity of making a difference is my great miracle. This paradigm pushed me into my launch onto my trek of life and purpose. As a result, I discovered insights and tools used to teach others on how to break from the illusions of lostness and lack of purpose. I *rose* above the clouds to an eternal perspective of seeing I was never lost; and to remember my truth and befriend my Ideal Self, who is the safe keeper of my purpose.

We are miracles, and every one of us has a journey. *I am* discovering mine. We are ever evolving infinite beings on a journey of love. I am privileged to be in a place to hear the call and jump for the opportunity to assist anyone who I am asked to participate in the adventure toward their personal transformations, spreading their wings and flying high to see how, and who, God sees through eternities. The horizon is limitless as are the possibilities ahead!

Chapter Three:

My Vision and Plan – *Root, Rebound, and Rise*

*"Nearly all men can stand adversity,
but if you want to test a man's
character, give him power."*
— Abraham Lincoln

T he call to create *The Triangle of Mastery's 7 Steps to Root, Rebound, and Rise* came as tragedy hit my hometown in 2017. The raging inferno, named the Thomas Fire, ravaged the hills of Ventura County, California. Then before we had a chance to recover from what was lost, the Woolsey Fire of 2018 cleared the remaining mountains as it took thousands of homes and structures with it. When all was done, many lives were lost, and eighty-three percent of the mountains were scorched.

I pondered life as I sat in midst the ruins left, reminded of the cleansing power of Mother Earth from the ground up. Through further reflection, the *7 Steps of Root, Rebound, and Rise* came to me as an answer to re-instilling resilience to our community. These 7 Steps came to me from a still, small voice of the whisperings from within my being incorporated in the following principles: *root, rejuvenation, real-I-zation, renew, revive, restore,* and *resurrection.* This is how the spirit speaks to my heart so there was no doubt I was being called to action and needed to listen. The *7 Steps of Root, Rebound, and Rise* bring together all these healing modalities for gaining mastery of the greatest obstacle we combat, Post Traumatic Stress Disorder (PTSD). As research is evolving on PTSD, we are discovering how each of us experience trauma throughout our growing years of life. The newest research recognizes the value of confronting the ramifications of developmental trauma quickly and thoroughly to ensure the opportunity to resolve our losses, untethered from the past, and be free to live in the present so we can show up for our future dreams come true. Upon further reflection, I could recognize that I had been prepped for this vision over the three decades plus of my career. This was most evident, as the population coming through my doors were specifically seeking refuge and reprieve from the newfound contention within their marriages, all synchronizing with the growing tragedies within our communities.

The Las Vegas Route 91 mass shooting (in 2017) that took fifty-eight lives, followed by the Borderline Bar shooting in my home town (in 2018), were surreal and beyond comprehension in and of themselves, all amidst Mother's Earths' scorching inferno, which, overloaded the coping circuits of the individuals throughout the community. Everyone was impacted by these calamities and their emotional reservoirs depleted quickly. Then, as they sought comfort within their marriage, they were met with further broken and fracturing attempts to reach back. Everyone's love buckets were empty from leaking out the holes shot through them or burnt away from the fires. They had nothing to give to one another, let alone keep for themselves. Hence, the timing of this revelation was clear to me.

Believing we learn more concretely and succinctly through symbols and rituals, I have packaged the *7 Steps of Root, Rebound, and Rise* in a symbolic matrix that came to me in a vision while under hypnosis. I call this *The Mastery of Triangle,* as it speaks to the mending of the heart in companionship of our Creator's covenant to being with us along our trek in life. As we accept His fullhearted outreaching hand to lead us, all healing and clarity comes, and purpose will be shown to us according to our faith in our purpose as co-creators. Again, we are not an island to ourselves, nor do most of us seek to be. As we implement these steps in our day-to-day lives and relationships, we mature into our Ideal Selves with the desire and ability to show up, serve, and love. By takeing one step at a time, we learn there is endless room at the top for all to *rise* and actualize where an evolved difference is made. This structuralizing matrix metamorphized as I worked with my clients. Their presented past traumas and the cycle that entrapped them were a catalyst that spurred some deep thinking. As more and more couples expressed conflict that was intertwined with the complexities of PTSD, it became apparent they were buried in a cycle of one crisis after another to the depths where they were unreachable and unresponsive to traditional talk therapy. The work done in the artificial setting of my office rarely proved to be transferable once they were back in their familiar paradigm that was tormenting them and led them to me in the first place. Despite the reprieve expressed and experienced within the four walls of my office, they continued to diminish as they re-entered their lives. They had no foundation to root, no tools to rebound, and no vision to *rise*. Hence, their lives represent the triangle pointing to the heavens and the first 3 steps of evolution (*re-awaken, rejuvenation and real-I-zation*). This triangle is the foundation gained from the therapy so that the work can begin. This beginning occurs as they exit their therapeutic endeavors. The goal of therapy is to engage the heart. It is the heart that becomes the bonding tie of commitment to *renew* via the Ideal Self, bridging the foundational work to the marvelous inner healer discovered within the higher realms of self-discovery. This is represented by the inverted triangle (*restore, resurrect and rise*) or God reaching down with His heart. Hence, the Triangle of Mastery reminding us that we are built for change, progression, and miraculous actualization with its endless and everlasting abundance of joy and love for healing.

As my clients and I exited the talking room, we put our hands in the dirt and dug into root, rebound, and *rise.* We danced, breathed, and mindfully maneuvered through barriers of the past and evolved through miracles, purging their untouched pain, while letting go of previous resistance and inhaling the fresh air of hope.

Once my clients *rose* with *renewed* hearts, they could breathe life back into their relationship and together engage in creative imagination to create a new blueprint of intimacy. I discovered that my couples proved to be highly responsive to learning and growing outside the therapy room and re-uniting by embracing *The Triangle of Mastery's 7 Steps of Root, Rebound, and Rise*. This work opened the way for them, individually and collectively, to conquer the trauma cycle and re-discover their true passion for one another.

For a couple to begin to break the bonds of trauma, they must first move forward starting with the foundation and flow in unison with the laws of nature and God, that is root, rebound and *rise*. We start where you are at. The transcending begins with waking up by opening the energy paths that are blocked by the absorption of traumas that occurred. One analogy used to walk clients through the *7 Steps to Root, Rebound, and Rise* is correlating them with the Chakras. Chakras are power centers in the body. There are seven main Chakras most popularly addressed that align with the base of the spine to the crown of the head. The word Chakra originates from the Sanskrit language, referring to a wheel or disk. These *wheels* are described as energy disks throughout the body and are used to help one connect with the body. I use the Chakras to assist in communicating within yourself as you navigate the seven steps of working through trauma and becoming your Ideal Self. As the Ideal Self is the celestial being within, the pure communication is through energy fields of the Chakras. The flow of energy traveling through the seven steps correlate with our Chakra powers and works through the invisible vehicle of breath, inspiration, and wisdom, which brings vibrance, life, and joyous love.

As we engage our energy and power through the healing of the trauma, the dance becomes visible and we are able to take the steps to releasing the bonds that hold us hostage to our past. We break through the interference to the present, opening to the future and manifesting as dreamed. In the chapters ahead, I take you through the steps of *The Triangle of Mastery's 7 Steps to Root, Rebound, and Rise*. In Chapter Five, I lead you to identifying where you start. The first step is to *re-awaken* and unearth yourself from being buried alive by the past traumas that have impacted you, defined you, and now taken your breath away. As you rediscover your foundation, stand on your two feet, and root into Mother Earth, you have the strength and support to re-capture your life. This step incorporates the *Muladhara,* root Chakra, or the energy vortex that represents where you came from and now where you are starting from. As you stand tall you are positioned to re-ignite this energy wheel, you *re-awaken* just as you did when you took your first breath and took accountability for the journey ahead. You are now in charge of the rest of your life.

We arrive to this earth fresh from the womb of our mother, pure and eager to embrace life. When hard knocks take us down time after time, we can become buried alive. *Rising* above the rubble of devastation and loss offers a re-birth and a second chance to build the life of your dreams. To *re-awaken*, we begin from the foundation up as the *Root* Chakra's energy vortex strengthens our stance, giving us foundational blueprinting to build strength and steadiness to move forward. As we stand on our own two feet, welcoming the life force of prana and embracing life with courage and boldness, we are taking accountability for each step forward. With a new beginning comes new awareness, a new innocence is born ready for the inner healer to guide you through the journey ahead. As you commit to yourself to begin, start where you are at and let the burning desire for breaking free flow through this vortex to re-invigorate the courage that is whispering from within. The is the *rooting* of commitment and accountability that fuels the faith to move through the muck to get to the horizon where your destination awaits you.

In Chapter Six, you will *rejuvenate* by learning how the dualities in your life are your playground where you learn to become. Unfortunately, we tend to be indoctrinated by our tribe from the get-go and fail to learn that we were meant to embrace what works for us as we live God's will, and what is meant to be discarded. This inhibits the differentiation process of evolving into our Ideal Self. Instead we get trapped into the pseudo-self that fits what we perceive the way to live. As we rejuvenate through an awareness of accountability within our inter-relational connections, we begin to witness the magic of diversity that is needed to flow forward in love and joy. The energy vibration of the *Svadhisthana,* or the Sacral Chakra, breaks down the old and welcomes the new, offering a *rejuvenation* for beginning anew. This second step represents all dualities in our lives, including the workings from within. We can see the grand design of duality between the dance of the body and breath, as seen within the first breath of life's agreement with the body to live life. It is here you may begin observing your own story that you brought with you as you infuse your breath, sounds, and vibrations on your new intentions. These stirrings of creativity encourage the rising of your truths and the intuitive awareness that catapults you forward in new beginnings and discovery of mind opening insights for further growing.

Once your being is re-energized with prana energy and your body is inflated to its potential height and breadth, you can *be* strong, courageous, and whole. You will learn to continue to *rejuvenate,* opening the energy voltage to ignite the passions and sensualities of the spirit and the body. It is here where you can then know where and who to show up as to achieve the unity you desire. Synchronically and simultaneously, you are stepping forward, embracing accountability for your life and then embracing the yin-yang connectedness which empowers you to create a life bond with your spouse in which you are free to love as desired. The energies can then can join and engage with one another to share in the mutual giftings of energy of duality. It is through duality that the self is reflected back to us to see, as we are mirrors for one another, providing insight and feedback on how we show up in this life. This continuous source of awareness provides opportunity for gaining information for our purpose so that we can evolve. Therefore, as you can see, marriage does not make you whole. The purpose of duality, the purpose of your marriage, is to have another with whom you share your completeness. It's a celebration of two Ideal Selves melding together to ignite the energies and spread the power of love for a more joyous journey together.

Hence, the work from our duality reflection provides a cleansing action, which helps increase life force/breath in your being. This works as a catalyst to remind you to continue the process with every step toward getting a grip of your PTSD and showing up in your relationships.

Chapter Seven addresses the third step: *Real-I-zation*. It is here that we take the captured reflections from others of the *I am* of who we are today. Through these reflecting images, messages, and energies we can learn which self is showing up, our pseudo-self or our Ideal Self. We resonate our individuality from our Solar Chakra or *Manipura*, which is located in the center of our body just above our navel. As we interact with one another, we intuitively sense how to show up and intimately relate to enhance our connections. As we come to know who we are showing up, we can *real-I-ze* who we want to become. We now have a compass for directing us where, how, and when to *be* so our Ideal Self can surface and direct us in the name of joy and love.

Born with the veil of forgetfulness from our eternal existence, we *awaken* in life situations where we absorb all that comes our way like sponges over the first three years of our life. As a result, we become potentially vulnerable to experiences and stimulations that are formative, loving, joyous, and sometimes traumatic to our soul. These early, transforming experiences lull us to or from becoming our Ideal Selves, and if distracted from our eternal purpose, we are vulnerable to being slowly molded into a pseudo self-engulfed in a variety of traumas through the course of our life. As you evolve from your tribal upbringing, learn from the reflected images and experiences of duality, you are ready to leave the nest and step into your autonomy embracing your differentiation and individuality. In other words, you are entering the world to be-ing, you learning and gaining the necessary *real-I-zations* of who you are.

This awareness includes knowing where you begin and end. That is, who you are in your wholeness and fragmented self. This is the step that offers insight as to how your trauma may have impacted your life's perceptions and choices and the insight for freeing yourself from the shackles of the armor casing previously created to keep you safe from your unbearable wounds. It is your personal energy and the continuous flowing that invigorates and cleanses your mind, body, and heart. Your gut is where your sense of Self resides. As you integrate the sensations from this area of your body and your mind, you will connect with a *knowing* or *real-I-zation* as *I am that I am,* thus a symbol of conquest and personal power firing up your new beginnings. The fire is the fuel igniting your inner healer or your Ideal Self, as this is area of your body where your identity resides.

It is here your body integrates the sensations with the *knowing*. Notice your feeling in the area of the body when you give it choices over the matter in which you have a dilemma. A sinking or nauseated feeling may indicate your decision is wrong, while a lightness may give a sense of rightness in your decision. As you successfully get to know your Ideal Self, you will gain the clear sense of direction to move forward in combatting your trauma that blocks your way from deciding how to show up for life and marry in alignment with your true essence.

As we evolve into being our Ideal Self, the Heart Chakra, or *Anahata,* lights up to *renew* the broken-heartedness to set you free. The heart holds the power of love, which is unquenchable abundance within each of us. Due to past traumas, the light can be dimmed and even blown out, yet the seeds of charity, although may feel dormant of emotion, are eternal. As you evolve out of your trauma, the personal stories of brokenness and unresolved grief can remain, preventing harmony from resolving past experiences. As the heart fertilizes the seeds of love, the *renewing* process is ignited and the unquenchable love banks from within to bathe you in the charity of all eternities.

Stress, trauma, and the difficult times do rear their heads and leave an imprint on us. It's the lasting negative experiences that attach to us, closing our heart as the aching and breaking feels too much. Fear replaces love, overshadowing the Ideal Self and shutting down any healing. This creates a deterioration, and the trauma chokes the life out of you, leaving an incomplete version of yourself, your pseudo-self.

Your heart is the place of your empathic center of expression, and the abundance of everlasting charity and joy reside in the heart center where love begets love. It is here you will learn to re-connect to the natural expansion of the heart, infuse your love with your partner, and encourage the synergy from within to without in a rhythmic dance of unity for everlasting healing.

In Chapter Eight, we *revive* our gift of free will while standing up and *voice our choice,* to further wash the past attachments to the pains of trauma. It's the contract to our Ideal Self to *rene*w your relationship from wirthinyour heart, allowing you to reclaim the love from within. As you engage in this introspective awareness, you open your capacity to feel your body and make good choices based on a deeper self-understanding. In turn, this reduces emotional reactivity, and combined with a little practice and the right tools, you can turn the hard times into victories.

Vishuddha, known as the Throat Chakra, *revives* the spark of your soul's mission; emphasis on showing up allows you to exercise one of the greatest gifts in life – that is your free will. We express our choices by using our voices. As your voice sounds its vibrational spark, you can be heard. Free agency is a recognition that you are taking a stand and actively participating in your life. You are shedding any last remnants that have enslaved you to the victim archetype or crippled you from knowing who you are to make life happen. By taking ownership of this eternal and innate right, we come to know that the happenings in life cannot take the Ideal Self-identity away from us. Life and people may detour us and create complexities and trauma, yet we have the ultimate choice as how we get a grip and *rise* above it. When acting on the gift to make a choice, we are *reviving* our sense of freedom, especially when faced with hard and painful matters, and claiming our power of manifesting faith, hope, and charity. This *reviving* paradigm shifts us into higher consciousness of inspiration free from constraint of worldly agendas and all choice in the *now*, unattached from the complexities of the past and the fears of the unknown. The only agenda is to love.

Chapter Nine looks to bring the upper Chakras in sync with the *restoring* power from within. Once the heart is engaged in the healing, the soul seeks to know what do with the freedom from being untethered from the past and the new released love expressed as a means of restoring your vision to our eternal purpose. Now that you are renewed and revived, you can be restoring to your purpose. This sixth step, *restore,* occurs as your purpose is rising to the surface. This is the Third Eye Chakra, known as *Ajna.* It is my belief we are all endowed with a purpose. Unfortunately, as we may get lost in the storms of life, we lose sight of having any purpose or fear our sense of purpose has been lost or we are mistaken. This step is the process of *restoring* your awareness and refining your skill of intuition. We all have intuition; as we evolve out of the pseudo-self and embrace the Ideal Self, we tap into our inner vision, seeing beyond the limited beliefs that interfere with reclaiming our celestial powers and *re-awaken* to an understanding and forgiveness of a mature soul. While we embrace the freedom to speak up and begin to make choices to support our Ideal Self, our power of discernment *rises* to our awareness. In turn, our insight sharpens, and we remember that we know more than we know we know. From here, reflection on all that was prior to the broken stories and hurts opens the mind to envision the golden nuggets amidst the hard knocks of life. You are now armed with the wisdom and clear vision to act on what you know and where you go.

Now unburied from the debris of past trauma, you see life clearly and discern intuitively how to create the life of your choosing. Self-reflection comes easily now and so does how to visualize the decision dream of your heart. While beginning to imagine how to cross the bridge of transformation in your marriage and hope unites what once was fractured, together you are aligned stronger and wiser than before.

In Chapter Ten, step Seven, *resurrect,* represents our arrival of coming from the place of knowing or wisdom. *Resurrection* has less to do with what you can do and more to do with what you are. From this view point, we transcend the struggles, disappointments, and troubles all of us have witnessed from an eternal perspective. As Josh McDowell shares in his quote in reference to Christ's *resurrection*, "The *resurrection* promises you a future of immeasurable good."

Resurrect correlates with the Crown Chakra located at the crown of our head, known as *Sahasrara*, which refers to being one with God in mind, body, and heart. It's like pulling back the veil, remembering who you are and recognizing the intelligence that truly runs the show. We essentially work through the sixth sense, our organic magnetic sense that we use in our evolution. It is what keeps us alive and surviving from the ground up. As we assimilate each step preceding our *resurrection*, we are prepared to manage the added insight, intellect, and expansion of the mind. As the mind expands and joins with the body and heart, its tripling force empowers us with the power to see what once was lost.

The Ideal Self embodies the mind-body-heart unity, expanding awareness and transcending from the gross matter of your physical presence to the subtler openings of your true intelligence, where wisdom is put into action of knowing. Seeing the world with *renewed* perspective allows for a paradigm shift in which you allow a vast connection between your innermost self and all things.

A paradigm shift is achieved, and the possibilities to life present as *now* you are present. *Re-awakening* to *resurrecting* has earned you the honor to access the way toward achieving your ultimate goal to *rise*.

I believe we are all called to *rise* to the occasion. And what is the occasion we *rise* to? You live your truth, now as your Ideal Self. I equate this to the evolving from the Star Chakra, known as *Padak-Pancaka*, on up. These are power centers to love beyond (the inspiration behind the creating to my coaching company, *to love and beyond)* our finite realm, as this is where we commune in a deep union with our Creator. This celestial realm is the place of infinity that carries the aura of Christ. It is here that we achieve the ability to love completely and fully with no attachment to understand. With this evolutionary key in hand, your Ideal Self can open the door to the treasured tool chest that manifests what it takes to join and reunite as one with your partner.

Just as science has shown how the body regenerates by growing new cells every seven years, we are capable of rising to love and going beyond the past trauma and multi-generational patterns to forgive and re-ignite the passion in the marriage again.

Here, tapping into your gratitude from the center of our heart, you reach the regenerative love and joy of the cocooning process of becoming. As you *rise* to become, you can transcend the barriers of time and tap into your Book of Life or Akashic records where your blueprint purpose is manifested between your immortal soul and your earth-bound personality. As you manifest your Ideal Self and commune with your Inner Healer, you *are* gratitude, love, and joy, which are the true healing elements. As a new day dawns, you *rise,* and your light shines, giving back by wrapping these rays around all who cross your path towards their wholeness. The evolution deepens your capacity to love and cherish with a *renewed* understanding of your and others' heart's intent. This understanding is absorbed into you becoming true to your Self by expanding your ability to see as your Creator sees, magnifying the healing process of remembering your eternal intelligence and grasping the lessons to be learned from every earthly experience as each soul plays its own important role in our interpersonal connections in life. And this extends to the most important relationship in your life, re-kindling the love and re-igniting the passion in your marriage, as well as evolving your union toward a celestial and everlasting happily ever after story.

Each of the above-explained steps are laid out in the *The Triangle of Mastery* diagram, which, can be found at my website, aplace2turn.com. Download the Free companion PDF to this book for a visual reference and as a blueprint mapping your personal evolution through the *7 Steps to Root, Rebound, and Rise*.

Chapter Four:

To Love... & Beyond

*"The only way to discover the limits
of the possible is to go beyond them
into the impossible."*
— Arthur C. Clarke

M y own story inspired me to write this book,
yet it's my clients who were the catalysts.
Through the years, my clients have asked
me to develop a formula they could work with between
our meetings to act as a compass to help them stay on
track. The work we do together is highly intuitive and
personally designed, giving it the power to create true
change in making their dreams come true.

I have identified the work we do in cognitive terms
and come up with seven steps that successfully resonate

the marvelous work done and the healing achieved. I am forever indebted to all the couples I have worked with through the years. Their willingness to be vulnerable and walk through the steps were inspiring in and of itself. Little did I know I would be witnessing miracles as the of vision these 7 steps came to life and are now the destination of getting a grip of their PTSD and saving their marriage.

I'm excited to share these steps upfront, as I believe they will be the kickstart to your success, happiness, and becoming whole and united. *The Triangle of Mastery* came to me in a vision during my hypnotherapy training. This self-hypnotic experience visited my endless broken heartedness that resonated with the fracturing burnt into my chest, paralyzing my ability to be personally vulnerable and blocking my intuitive connection in my life.

In the illuminous state, I was able to *re-awaken* to an understanding that I had a major role in staying brokenhearted and barricading myself from connecting with others heart to heart. This proved to be an epiphany, which *rejuvenated* my hope and curiosity in what would my life be like if I burst through the barricades and lived boldly. This *real-I-zation* did not rectify itself all at once. Yet what I did get was this vision of the blueprint of *The Triangle of Mastery*. As time went forward, this vision of *The Triangle of Mastery* stayed present with me, and I knew that I had to resolve the sadness to manifest the purpose behind this vision. It came during another training, this time for Eye Movement Desensitization Reprocessing Therapy (EMDR). As part of the training, we participate as the client. Although I picked a benign memory and cognition to work on, my mind took me to the origin where my heart broken. As I held on and breathed through the free falling of letting go of what was no longer needed, I literally broke through my rusty armor, and my heart was *renewed* instantaneously. I woke up to a heart free from the decades-long companionship of the aching that barricaded my love from within.

This freedom was like a breath of fresh air as I experienced an inner cleansing that *revived* me from the dead. I was alive again and free to choose how to show up, ready to cocoon for complete transformation, and simultaneously manifesting the purpose I was being drawn toward. It was at this time the values which support *The Triangle of Mastery* appeared. I could see with eyes of wisdom that was beyond my earthy acquiring. This is when my power of discernment became prominent and the lesson from my ancestral heritage could be witnessed. I was not alone. I then found myself at another training for Quantum Energy Healing where I learned to embrace my energy field (we all have one), *restoring* my empathic nature fully, and flew to new heights with witnessing others' stories and identifying their needs to manifest the marvelous miracles from that time forward.

I had *resurrected* from the cocoon and was free to see from the perspective from above, which, is now the imagery for *To Love… & Beyond*. This led me to my final journey of *The Triangle of Mastery* trek as I landed in the world of yogis. Indulging in the Yoga teacher training as an adjunct to assist others in shedding the remnant of trauma stored in their body turned to be my piloting school, in which my original vision showed herself as the model of guiding all to *rising* above their trauma. Hence, the marriage of *The Triangle of Mastery* to the 7 steps to *Root, Rebound, and Rise* manifested into becoming the path of rediscovering your marriage as you successful rising from your PTSD.

So, the journey begins.

First, it's important to know your enemy and gain some awareness of the many faces of trauma and an understanding of what is Post Traumatic Stress Disorder. For years, PTSD was reserved for those exposed to war, violence, or terrorism. Today, this definition has been expanded to include overexposure to experiences that are interpreted by our brains as being toxic, insulting, disturbing, and other negative experiences which leave a negative imprint on our mind, body, and spirit. This added definition has become known as Complex Trauma, as it describes exposure early in life which disrupts our development and formation of any sense of self. Children who experience interference with forming trusting relationships can end up with inhibited secure attachments. As adults, this can manifest in building an armor of protection from those most intimate in our world, hence disrupting the growth of a marriage in every way.

As a clinician, I use the Diagnostic and Statistical Manual of Mental Disorder V (DSMV) to diagnose clients and assess the best course of treatment. One colleague noted that if we took all the diagnosis outlined in the manual and funneled them all down to one diagnosis, it would be unresolved grief. This resonated with me as I reflected on the thousands of clients in my practice, underneath every symptom and behavior which came into the room with them was a story of unresolved loss. This loss creates a breach of trust, many times beginning from the youngest of memories to the more recent, presenting problems, which, brought them to me.

I quickly learned that discharging the trauma was not enough, as most times it only addressed the symptoms, and the void of connecting and attaching becomes most apparent, thwarting further healing. Without addressing the mind, body, and heart from the bottom up, only surface resolution is achieved. Many times, the trauma remains deep within the cells of the body and within the soul. This leaves one vulnerable to cycling back in various trauma states as new challenges, trials, and tribulations come along the way. The evidence of the unresolved healing tends to manifest in the intimate relations where connections become frayed as the inner chaos works to wear down any resilience and endurance. When we are broken down, there is a tendency to resort to our lowest denominator of coping. The pseudo-self makes a good effort, yet her resources are limited to the way it was done in the past, as no future vision is within her reach. Hence, unintentionally, the trauma cycle repeats and then can recreate the nightmare you just evolved from.

The Triangle of Mastery captures the full realm of healing from creation to eternal destination. As the *7 Steps to Root, Rebound, and Rise* are followed, each step addresses a deeper layer of your being, making sure no *T* is left uncrossed. In the book *Getting Well Again*, author O Carl Simonton, M.D., shares how cancer patients went into complete remission with hypnosis. However, while fifty percent experienced healing, fifty percent died. To understand how come half the patients went into remission, and the other half did not, they repeated the hypnosis treatment. This time, they had the patients draw a picture of their hypnotic vision. The same results occurred with these patients. As they reviewed their drawings, they learned that every patient who lived cleaned their cancer out completely, and every patient who died left a trace of cancer behind. Some left a mere dot on the page, yet left in place, the dis-ease took over. This is a perfect analogy of what occurs when one works *The Triangle of Mastery* and when one merely addresses the symptoms. The trauma must be thoroughly explored to be understood, handled with care to gain the lesson to be learned, and then the unnecessary pain expunged.

As you continue the trek of evolution, clarity manifests into lessons and then trauma can be experienced as transforming you toward *be*-ing your Ideal Self, gifting you a glimpse of the diamond in the rough. A diamond is a piece of charcoal that handles trauma exceptionally well, and in that source of trauma is the refining fire for the healing. As outlined in my journey, *The Triangle of Mastery* is the molding energy, which, leads to *letting go*, and releasing stress and trauma from your mind, body, and spirit. With each step you discharge the energy that was mobilized for fight/flight/freeze mode of operation, which, the past trauma triggers. On the other hand, if you choose to not step up, you become vulnerable to falling into a dissociative state, and over time, you are susceptible to collapsing under the weight of the disturbance, trapping the very pain of it all. By venturing through the *Root, Rebound, and Rise* steps, you tap into "muscle memory" held deep within your reserves managed by your Inner Healer. As I learned from my search for modalities most effective in getting a handle on PTSD, I found there is only one way, and that is moving from the inside out. The development of the *7 Steps to Root, Rebound, and Rise* takes you through the inner journey, in which, you can reach the crippling complexities of past traumas stored in the deepest regions of the mind, body, and spirit, and step into the healing matix.

Metamorphically, the inner healer is found within the power centers of the body known as the Chakras. When in tune with your inner healer, you can mend each wound, nourish each depletion, and re-ignite each breath of life. The *7 Steps to Root, Rebound, and Rise* is associated with a Chakra power center, showing you how to tap into your own energy field to become whole again. This is reached by working beyond the talk about the stories of the battle between the perpetrator and victim. The realm of the inner healer is the quiet within you; this vibrational tone is the whisper of the message of peace to the mind, body, and spirit. This musical sound overrides the noise of the trauma. As you take each step, contemplate your evolution, you begin to meditative acquaint with your Ideal Self, at which time, you may join in prayerful communion with your Creator, where you can hear and experience the resonating and energetic vibrations for healing. You mind expands, and you can remember you are more than this earthly presence and your purpose becomes clear.

A new perspective arises, and you begin to recognize your mission has a duality or opposite in all things; own the *I am* that makes your calling your calling; express gratitude from the heart as you tap into your eternal fountain of love; know how to speak your truth; sharpen your discernment and develop a laser clarity of seeing beyond the stars in the sky, you *be*-come one in mind or your Ideal Self, as the eternity awaits you.

Now that you have the end in mind, you can step to the starting line, starting where you are at. Before I walk you through the *7 Steps to Root, Rebound, and Rise*, I am going to introduce you to the tools and modalities that led to the discovery and magic *of The Mastery of Triangle*.

Maslow's Hierarchy of Motivation is what I consider a preliminary tool that provides a good explanation as to what motivates for change. In 1943, Abraham Maslow wrote a paper proposing "A Theory of Human Motivation," which grew into the observations of our innate curiosities and needs for motivation. To see a color illustration of Maslow's creation, download the free companion PDF to this book at aplace2turn.com.

Maslow's work reiterates the need to work from the ground up, meeting our basic survival needs for sustenance and drive to obtaining food and shelter before we can consider any other need. The action to step up and ask for help begins the dual interaction, where we then can give back. It is in the interaction with the world where we seek safety and security, and as we become stabilized, we are more inclined to seek a sense of belonging and connecting with another. Once the heart bonds with others, our esteem grows, and we establish values and shared beliefs. As we practice these values and expand our beliefs, we experience motivation to self-actualize into our Ideal Self.

This was my first introduction to the power of symbols in providing a roadmap to personal growth and maturing. Maslow's hierarchy resonated with me as I reflected on my own attraction and attachment to symbols and rituals, as we all are. Like many, I just hadn't recognized how my collections of rabbit foot good luck charms, trolls and pressed flowers were symbols that helped form my values. Nor did I appreciate the interactive play with my baby dolls, stuffed animals, and roly-poly bugs provided as ritual protypes for future interpersonal connections. The power behind learning through symbols and rituals than talking is it brings about life-altering change more permanently. By taking it to heart and testing this theory, and I became a believer. So, no wonder my vision manifested its messages through symbols and rituals that evolved into these steps of self-mastery!

As a variety of tools are useful navigating through the seven steps, I will take a moment to define and explain some of the more effective therapeutic techniques:

Hypnotherapy directs you to the natural yet altered state of mind which connects with your inner healer and facilitates change at the deep levels where your beliefs reside. The therapist assists the client in accessing these inner resources for solving challenges and *rising* above and beyond the complexities of your PTSD more easily. It has been shown that through hypnosis the client's creative imagination is accessed and the subconscious thought processes are opened. Hence, the avenues and depths for healing become infinite as hypnotherapy has brought about breakthroughs for lasting growth.

Heart Math is a science-based meditation technique focusing on placing your attention to the heart and breathing from your heart center. You breathe a little more deeply than usual and express your heart felt appreciations from the inside out, imagining it is through the heart. This is what I discovered to be the home of your inner healer who opens the path to increasing your energy, gratitude, and endurance by joining through the heart-focused breathing.

Eye Movement Desensitization Reprocessing (EMDR)Therapy has been coined "magical", as this bilateral movement technique effectively leads to healing your trauma by opening your transpersonal experience and your spiritual areas, including, but not limited, to the development of wisdom, compassion, trust in life, forgiveness, insights, epiphanies, experiences of spiritual freedom, and openings into the psychic realm.

Quantum Energy Healing is modality that teaches you to get in touch and familiar with your personal vibrational energy. As you master the ability to communicate with the energy you are, you will be better able to cross your transformational bridge, joining with your wisdom of knowing on an inspirational wavelength to reach your desired peace and self-love and love of another.

Reiki Healing is another energy healing modality. Reiki, which means universal life force energy, is a laying on of hands touch healing system. It's known for having incomparable ease and power in bringing one to a sense of union and oneness with all being.

Self-Compassion and Trauma Recovery Yoga. Self-compassion has been shown to be a most effective strategy for making behavioral changes towards transformation from the negative patterns of your saboteur. Healing through movement reconnects you with the rhythm and vitality of life as you learn to be gentle and accepting in working for change. Self-compassion will be your greatest source of strength in understanding the mind, body, and spirit connection as movement works to establish a greater sense of being balanced, grounded, and at ease. As a science-based somatic method, yoga is integrated with proven techniques to inspire a sense of safety and connection. Lastly, yoga builds up resourcing within the body, which helps to tolerate your sensations and to regulate.

Symbols are used to teach how to draw from Mother Earth and learn self-healing via her creations, energy forces, and regenerative capacities – crystals, tree of life, wisdom of your animals, and much more.

Writing and Re-writing your Story is the power of journaling with the purpose of showing up in the expression of your words.

Art Therapy via drawing, coloring, painting and more teaches you to step aside and allow your unconscious creations to surface and speak the messages you are learning *now* to create your healing path.

Sound, Aroma, Water, and Movement Therapies. This is raising the five senses to open the way for your sixth sense, intuition, and inspiration to show up, be heard, and work the magic of maturing into your eternal being. Yoga, especially, teaches you to breathe life back into the body and exfoliates past trauma from our physical body at the cellular level. *Nature* is a healing vessel at everyone's disposal. When we take in breath, we are connecting with healing elements of Mother Earth. As designed, the plants and vegetation that beautify our surroundings are supported by the carbon dioxide we humans exhale. In turn, they give back not just with their beauty for our visual pleasure; they also exhale the oxygen we need for our sustenance. The definition of marriage can be the partnership modeled throughout the world of symbols and rituals, mirroring back who we are and offering support for where we desire to go.

As you can see, there are endless lists of modalities to work from. My hope is that by opening the door to possibilities, you enter into your personal exploration and use your creative imagination to design your course of maneuvering through the steps in this book. The discoveries can be found through one or many of these tools in which your conscious mind steps aside for the inner healer to *rise* and create a new paradigm free from the *stuckedness* of PTSD. As a child pretending in play and learning to interact with their world, you too can learn within your magical playground of pretend, filled with an array of toys, games, animals, and blossoming flowers of sweet fragrances.

These tools are magnificent, and when implemented with intention to heal, dedication to practice, and diligent effort, the path for healing is opened. As stated already, I use these tools myself and in my practice with clients. I have witnessed the miraculous evolution on both fronts. And now that you are aware of some tools – as there are an abundance out there to choose from – it's important that you understand their power and role in your healing. It's imperative you recognize that they are just tools, not the healers. They are at your disposal to assist you through the new territory you will be forging through to get to your destination. Each step that we walk through in this book is transformational in and of itself. As you truly work each step, using every tool at your disposal to get you through to the level of your inner healer, you will transform. There is no way not to, as your very intent to dig yourself out of being buried alive by the past will change the cells in your body. Again, as a man thinks, so he is. Then, as you continuously persist carrying forward your new awareness, knowledge and skill gained from each new step will set you free.

The Triangle of Mastery's 7 Steps to Root, Rebound, and Rise will set you free through self-awareness, so you know where to start, that is, where you are at and, then embrace the I Create and Achieve (ICAN) attitude to make your dreams come true. Getting to know your Ideal Self and marrying *The Triangle of Mastery* into your being, sets the prototype to saving your marriage. By walking through the *7 Steps to Root, Rebound and Rise*, you will be intuitively drawn to where to turn for wholeness, one step at a time. And as you experience the benefits of your hard work, a paradigm shift will happen, and you will see what you could not see before and be who you were not able to be before. Can you imagine breaking through your rusted armor, cocooning for transformation and strengthening your resolve to fly to greater heights, free from the tethering to your PTSD? Can you imagine choosing where to stand, how to show up in your relationship? Can you imagine being as you are? Can you imagine embracing the *I am* with you in the name of love? Can you imagine using your voice to freely express your choices? Can you imagine tapping into your unique intelligence with discerning clarity on how to keep yourself safe? And can you imagine living, breathing, and being your Ideal Self and being one with your Creator? You are as you were created to *be*. Now you are free to *rise* and then unite with your partner to create new beginnings for a happy ever after life. This journey will lead you on the way to being whole and creating a duality of wholeness. What are you waiting for? Begin now, by starting where you at, and move forward, one step at a time. By doing so from the inside out, you are united with your Ideal Self, and in "matrimony" guided through your course to *be*-come whole.

Chapter Five:

Re-awaken; Re-birth to Recreate

*"We think we're living in the present,
but we're really living in the past."*
— John Banville

A s the saying goes, you are the main actor in the story of your life. So, the best place to start from is where you are now. We come into this world alone, and we die alone, and we are eternally part of a larger family and community on both sides of the veil. As it appears, we are created to be one with another, and this is a key premise of my theory that on how true healing occurs. We are not an island to our-selves, so must learn to show up, move over, and be present with what we are given and whom we are to love. We simply cannot do that without knowing who we are first in mind, body, and spirit; then to use who we are to love one another. This momentum of energy is where the power of love ignites the true healing.

Step one, *re-awaken*, represents our beginning, which is now. We *re-awaken* to who we are today. As you will discover through this process, you are who you desire to *be*. As you take each breath, you are deciding to live your life, and this puts you center stage as the main character of your story. As we recognize that we are the author of our own story, we are *re-awakened* to the accountability for our part of the play, and empowered, as we take a stand to begin the journey for our personal evolution. As the main character, we are first and foremost responsible for the joy and love we bring to the story as well as the pain we are holding onto. You may want to put the book down right now as you did not and would not ask for the lack of joy and love in your life nor begin to even imagine the kind of misery you have been subjected. I get it. This may sound insensitive – that's not my intent – yet the truth does set us free. I have found in my work that healing cannot begin without taking accountability for our role in life first and foremost. Once we know where our own breath begins and ends, then we can expand to the rest of story. As we *re-awaken*, we must take a firm stand and root with conviction of being in our life story so that we can write the story of our dream come true now. This is the beginning of discarding the old patterns and breaking the grip of the past toward building our happily ever after fairytale of love.

So, you may then ask what this has to do with healing your marriage? The truth is everything, and at the same time, this is not a typical book on marriage; it's first and foremost about you. As you, the main star of the show, lead the way to collaboratively transforming and healing, all *rise* with you, evolving into a likeminded unity. To address the whole, we must address the parts, and as you come to know where you start, then you can also know where the source of the pain resides for you and the relationship. There are numerous reasons behind a divorce, yet the part you have control over is where your accountability lies. The challenge is to address your accountability for clarity, life learning and enlightenment, This, in turn, opens the way for extending mercy and love on what has occurred to free yourself to *be* and move forward. When one or the other or both in a marriage hold on to the past, consciously or unconsciously, it becomes a catalyst for pain and prevents growth and evolution. This unfinished state detains you and/or the relationship in turmoil that can result in PTSD. As a result, some marriages are not saved because one or both may be too traumatized to want change. Hence, they resort to divorce as the change, yet without being any closer to *re-awakening*, they are just as fractured as they were in their tumultuous union. When the choice to root and stand in being accountable is made, you can no longer be whipped around by the winds of chaos. Your roots provide stability from within, fortifying you to hold strong to who you are and where you begin. This accountability shields you from the ramifications of shame and guilt that are created when you follow the outside in to be wherever the whims of chaos take you.

As you stop and take this moment to take charge from within, discard the festering wounds from the past by writing a new story for the new day, and own your role and root to *re-awaken*, you will become whole. As you are whole, you are available to be present and pro-actively be in your relationship. This change is work and evolution. This means having to discard every reason or disguise for what currently is. And I have come to learn that as you follow these steps you will transform, and your marriage can follow. The purpose of addressing the marriage is because as relational beings we cannot escape *marriage* or affiliation with another. To isolate, we must have someone to isolate from and to bond we must have someone to bond with, hence the need for addressing the union in healing from our past trauma and the continuous PTSD fallout.

I hope to demonstrate throughout this book that as you shed your armor of protection and begin to see the *I am* beyond the trauma you can become personally vul-nerable to love. Love and fear cannot co-exist. Once you can love, you will no longer fear to own your role with full accountability; you will have no more attachment to your trauma and become free to love again. A paradigm shift will occur, and you will show up. You will see differently and come to know yourself as a lovable and valuable being. Your whole focus will shift from where you are to where you need to become.

Prashna Upnanshad's ancient story of the infamous debate between breath (prana or life force) and our five senses provides a good starting place to explain the relationship within ourselves between the pseudo-self and the Ideal Self. The story is that the prana spoke up, noting that none of the five senses could exist without it. The prana demonstrated its power by leaving the body. As professed, once prana left, the five senses grew weak. Once this truth was realized, the prana superiority was acknowledged, and the five senses apologized, bowing in honor to the prana.

The first thing that determines we have vitality is the breath we take as we come from the womb. This prana gives the very energy to our faculties; as we manage our faculties, we can then manage our life. Likewise, the Ideal Self is our master healer and carries the wisdom and holds the compass to navigate us through our life purpose, and the pseudo-self is the by-product of our allowance of life's happening to define us. When left without the Ideal Self, we are weakened and lost in the wilderness of chaos, as the pseudo-self is without understanding and has no compass. Our pseudo-self knows only to react to what comes its way, with no thought of proactive living or sense of purpose. This brings us to our first step to root so we can *rise*.

I ask you to reflect on where are you in relation to your pseudo-self. Taking this first step of positioning yourself as where you will place your feet to root for launching forward is a defining moment as if brings you to the present facing forward. It is here you are positioned to ask yourself, are you in alignment with living your purpose? And how, what, and where are you misaligned from your inner desires and passions for living and loving in every way? As you make the decision to take a stand to live what you know and continue to discover your Ideal Self, you are in place to learn the lessons you are positioned to learn as every lesson is vital and perfect for reaching to the destination you set out to do. The moment you root in place, you will know it, and things will start to fall into place; you become your purpose, and the old struggle lifts.

You are starting at a place where you have felt hopeless, buried alive by your PTSD, and losing the love of your life.

Know now, as you root into the ground of your purpose, hold on and watch for the wonderful changes to unfold, step by step and/or in a twinkling of an eye, you will reclaim *you*, and your marriage will follow.

Once the umbilical cord is cut and you take your first breath, you are accountable for each inhale and exhale thereafter. Accountability is an all-time and everlasting value. We take ownership from the get-go as we invite the life force to enter our body. Over time, your trauma may have frayed your tie to accountability for yourself and your sacred contracts.

Step one is to re-create a culture of accountability, starting with you. Standing in plain sight is your first commitment to being accountable, followed by walking the talk that keeps you present so you can *re-awaken* and be re-born. Now that you can walk, the challenge begins to stay off the spectator sidelines where you watch life pass you by. It is time to enter the game of life, ready to define who you are from this day forward. When accountable, you get to know your enemy fast and how furiously engaged he is with the pseudo-self and keeping you held hostage to your past trauma. This gives you the opportunity to decide to stand up and gain mastery of this pseudo-self or stay enslaved by the ignorance and suffocation of staying where you are. As you take ownership of your role as star actor in your story, you are positioned to see what is working for you and what is not and to know what is right and what is wrong. This opens the way to begin to start to figure out what change is needed to override your trauma and take command of your life. Again, our first breath is the taking ownership of our mind, body, and spirit, and accountability is established. It starts with you *now*.

The PTSD cycle entraps you by impeding you from creating and achieving your greatest fantasy you dreamed to being. All attempts for any intimate connection with the complexities of your traumas are sabotaged and robbing you of your life endeavors, including a marriage of love, sensuality, and happily ever after. The truth is unknowingly the pseudo-self has united with your PTSD, and, unfortunately, a marriage to your PTSD is the interference, as it creates a persona of *woundology,* coined by Carolyn Myss. Healing is believed to be achieved by wearing the armor of victimization, saboteur, and/or prostitute, to name a few. Archetypes, such as, these can shackle your psyche with a sense of learned helplessness and dilute your awareness that you have the power of personal accountability. Learned helplessness paralyzes you with emotions of guilt, blame, and shame, sending you into a state of overwhelming drive to escape life and all intimate connections, especially with the Divine. As a result, you become defined by these wounded archetypes and seek bonding via your past hurts, pain, and turmoil.

When embroiled in your PTSD, there is a tendency to continue to re-open those wounds long past the occurrence and then share them in every aspect of your life. In the beginning of healing, this is a stage of grief, yet there comes a point where personal accountability steps in and you must take charge of your own life again. If not, the relationship with *woundology* fosters patterns of re-exposing yourself to trauma and re-injuring you over and over.

As you remember your decision to stand on your principle of accountability for your life, you are taking the first step to breaking the trauma cycle and shedding the armor of debilitating archetypes which rob your power to show up.

I liken the analogy of the pebble in the palm of your hand to what it looks like to getting a grip of your PTSD and becoming free to stand on your own two feet. If you take a round, flat, quarter-sized pebble and place it in front of one eye as you close the other, all you can see is the pebble. It is the world presented to you. As you pull it away from your eye, it becomes smaller, and you see the world surrounding it. Then, as you place the pebble in the palm of your hand, you now have a grip on the what once was a visual barrier that seemed all-consuming.

You are not meant to stay wounded. You are meant to heal and transform.

Just as this analogy demonstrates, as you get a grip of your past traumas, you can see there is more on the horizon. And on the horizon, there is opportunity to love, ignite your passion, and create healthy marriages. Being the main character of your story, you do determine the intention of how your story plays out. As you embrace accountability by standing strong and readying yourself to take action, you are able to look to the road ahead, take hold of opportunities, and strategically determine *now* what you can do to embrace your inner healer, in which resides reflection and manifests vibrational energy for breaking from the stagnation of any remnants of *woundology*.

Our root Chakra *Muladhara* is said to be located at the base of the spine and considered the seat of the Kundalini, or power center for our energy force. In correlation with the first step to *re-awaken*, the Root Chakra represents our very survival instincts, self-preservation, trust, and safety. It is the gateway to claiming your right to be here, breathe life into your body, and nurture it through your first year.

Standing deeply rooted and claiming your place among your tribal family is Step 1. Here, you can create your intention to honor the breath that brought life to you. This alone is more healing than most realize. A small intention of gratitude opens the heart to an awareness of the capacity of the lungs – their dance offers an expansion of life through breath of depth and breadth. As our body synchronically breathes the dance of love, the healing begins – all from a mere intention to take accountability for inhaling the prana or life force of our inner healer, the Ideal Self – whereas life without reflection on your intention allows for the trauma to guide the pseudo-self according to its whim, making you vulnerable to being detoured from your life's path.

As we visited earlier, the law of nature incorporates an opposition in all things. It is your conscious intention and ownership in where your accountability lies that puts you in the driver's seat of navigating this mechanism of your desired plan. As you place your intention out to the universe and take on the ICAN attitude, you manifest your heart's desires. You take your golden nuggets from the past forward, show up as our evolving selves and breathe in life to stand tall and envision a future full of joyful unions ahead.

Our dreams are a great teacher of how to commune with our inner healer. As you ponder over a dream which left you with feelings of profound meaning for your life, this is likened to unlocking the communication with your Inner Healer. In the beginning, entering life is *re-awakening* to a foreign land, as the veil of forgetfulness gives us the impression that the first incident we confront is the trauma of the cutting of the umbilical cord. Our avenue for breath is shut off without a moment's notice. To live, we are faced with death – opposition in all things from the get-go. Only by embracing the new relationship with prana can life on earth begin.

So, you did this – you already took a stand by the very fact that you are alive. One step with the intent to live claimed your first experience of autonomy.

Most times we experience trauma without seeing the opposite reward in the moment. Having the awareness of this universal law and the faith in things not seen can provide a foundation for continuing to breathe in prana with the added intent of the ICAN approach to seeing what you want to see, hearing what you want to hear, and knowing what you want to know. Then hope can bud from the seeds of your faith and charity blossoms from within where healing occurs. Thus, your relationship with your Ideal Self begins to unfold and presents the prototype to bridge the intimacy back into your earthly relationships, beginning with your marriage.

As you struggle in your journey and question why you are feeling stuck in life, hitting roadblocks, and experiencing challenge after challenge, you may wonder why you can't manifest the life of your dreams. This could be the very ingredient missing in your life: your dreams.

Dreams can be *the* place to receive guidance directly from your Ideal Self, as well as, offer insight on how to hear the whisperings from within via listening to your intuition, answering your prayers, and acknowledging you know more than you know you know.

As you stand in the present, you are able to move past the whirling of your mind and hone the messages of higher truths, gaining the knowledge of what will set you free to set foot on your right path.

As you venture forth, *re-awakened* and newly acquainted with your inner healer, you are present to listen and gain the insights into your waking life that will lead you to opportunities for transformation, healing, and understanding what life will be like having gained mastery over your PTSD and being free to love again.

Consistent practice and effort are the secret behind creating and maintaining a new paradigm shift toward taking a stand for your life! Just as the butterfly in the cocoon strengthens her wings by pushing against the cocoon to crack it so she can fly, we, too can push against the impulses and urges from the PTSD to break free, springing forward and *rise* above it.

An analogy I am drawn to is from *The Karate Kid* where Mr. Miyagi instructs Daniel to wax his antique automobiles, with specific directions to use circular motion of *wax on...wax off...wax on...wax off...* He followed this up with more tasks, which entailed consistent practice and effort: sand the floor *side to side*; paint a fence *up and down...* Through these simple instructions, he was preparing Daniel to develop the skills to defend himself in karate. This mastery is the foundational step in the triangle of *rising* to your potential and heart's desire.

This begins with making the decision to show up and step up and then take accountability for follow through until the new skill is mastered. Daniel not only wanted to master his karate skills, he welcomed his mentor's wisdom and guidance. He lived the mantra, "It's better to be obedient than right." Then he accepted the directives and put forth the effort and consistent practice and created a win-win scenario for himself and his mentor.

As you break through your cocoon and master your ability to fly, you *re-awaken* the passion within your marriage. You and your spouse are then, free to *rise* to the great horizon ahead, both equally redirected, rooted, and accountable in creating your win-win formula hand in hand.

Standing your ground is the first step in achieving mastery as you make the commitment within and stick with it, no matter what bonds you must break, barriers you climb over and apron string you untangle from.

With consistent practice and effort, patterns reveal themselves in behavior changes and mastery, as the inner healer miraculously metamorphoses you into your Ideal Self.

As you can now see, our body's miraculous mechanism of breath is a prototype for taking in what is needed for life and expelling what is no longer wanted.

Once *re-awakened*, prana can then be used as the source of creative power as it is the expression of the master healer to work at every level of your being. This inner energy powers and transforms our consciousness and is key to unlocking your ability to break through the pseudo-self's sabotaging thoughts and feelings from your PTSD.

Standing strong is supported by working with your breath through specific breathing exercises known as pranayama. Pranayama is mostly taught in the support of yoga. Yoga emphasizes purification of the mind, body, and spirit with the goal of Self-realization, and recognizes the need to celebrate the life force by bringing it into your life and actions. Breath enlivens emotions of love, joy, and peace and releases fear, grief, and turmoil.

You are now ready to root with a strong foundation *to start where you are at* and move forward from this day forward.

To see a color illustration of *The Triangle of Mastery's Step 1: Reawaken*, download the free companion PDF to this book at aplace2turn.com.

Chapter Six:

Rejuvenate and Regenerate

*"Oh what a wonderful soul so bright
inside you. Got power to heal
the sun's broken heart, power
to restore the moon's vision too."*
— Aberjhani, Songs from the
Black Skylark zPed Music Player

I was standing on a small bridge in the middle of the mountain range of Are, Sweden. I set out in the wee hours of the morning for a run; as this was new country for me, exploration was on the agenda. I have a tradition of searching for bridges when I come to new places, as they are a symbolic vision of transformation in my imaginative world.

Finding the little bridge that hovered over a small creek, I stood in the middle and looked to the horizon, yet my attention immediately diverted to a tree standing directly in front of me. It rooted out from the center of the creek, planted with a three-foot round trunk which then sprung two separate trunks reaching to the sky. As I believe that when we are present and living with intention, we are presented symbols and signs offering insights and answers that leads us toward our desired destination. This tree caught my attention. I noted the symbolism of the trunk as it rooted in unity with mother earth, divided to becoming two of the same. As with the second Chakra, *rejuvenation* begins as you take this next step.

The second step, *rejuvenation* addresses the concept of duality and non-duality of life and it is represented in the reproductive region of your body where we carry the energy known as *Svadhisthana* or sweetness.

After *re-awakening, rejuvenation* occurs as we recognize duality and non-duality. We learn I am me and you are you and together we can *be* one. Just as this occurs when we leave the pre-existence and enter this life, a veil of forgetfulness separates us from our Creator. This tree reminded me that the division of the two trunks comes from a united foundation which never wavers despite the earthly vision limited to its finite realm.

The illusion of duality occurs as you identify with and/or attach to whirling of the mind. That is, the identifying with images and thoughts, which, arise from the content of one's conditioning over time. As you stand on the foundation of oneness, pure awareness's presence can be felt and heard through the veil, reminding you that you are truly never alone.

This in turn becomes your perception and then your paradigm of all that you experience in your life journey and you come to recognize time and space are an illusion. This opening to the eternities *rejuvenates* you as understanding expands to infinity and to both sides of possibilities along with it. This empowering revelation brings hope to the sad as its duality is happy; fear is one side of the coin, and love is its opposite.

Duality offers clearer insight that again brings you to a *renewed* awareness of the law of opposition in all things. To know peace, you must also know suffering. Therefore, holding onto pain cripples us and gives us more to the same; hence, we re-experience the very pain itself. As we embrace the duality and seek for the reflected opposite, we can *rise* beyond the pain to find soothing elements and relief. Then, as we walk through the journey to the end, we inevitably come to the healing and the lessons learned along the way. The truth that we are never given more than we can handle is lived, and we can sing, *oh, how true it is*! The icing on the cake is the introduction to the divine duality of our life process. As we look to every relationship – troubled or not – with infinite vision, we begin to break through the veil leading to pure consciousness of the divine. This purity offers insight to the further clarity about the heartbreaking confusion of opposition and offers greater creative means to incite the burning desire to seek, hear, and to know from here.

Realizations and awareness of your oneness with the Divine only occur in the clarity of the present moment – never in the past or future but only now. Put another way: In the present moment, clarity is. Not clarity was or clarity will be, as clarity is or is not.

Be-ing one with the Divine occurs in the present moment as duality melds into nonduality and you transcend the limitations of the mind into becoming your Ideal Self. Some refer to this as enlightenment, free from the attachments to finite stories. Whether coping with a broken heart or not, an eternal perspective offers a powerful position of being aware of the *now*. In the present moment, truth is.

As I stood on that small bridge that day, this is the message that was written on my heart. With the eternities opened to me, I embraced the lessons gifted from the tree that taught me duality and nonduality both exist. You start with you – where you are at *now* in relation to your world, and specifically your marriage. As you come together now, nonduality begins to show herself and bound the two of you into becoming as one. Want it to happen, then you can make it happen. As you stay in the now, you meld your hearts again, in a twinkling of an eye.

Just like that!

The Sacral Chakra symbolizes duality so well. As previously stated, its position in the body is below the navel, encompassing your reproductive organs, and could be said to represent your creative forces. You were born to live a human life experience yet are reminded that you are your Creator's creation. Hence, both body and soul unify here, mortality and divinity. Again, faced with choice, the dilemmas and lessons are deciphered here to learn to co-create with spirit.

The purpose of mortal life is to provide the experiences (peace and suffering) needed to live your purpose as you simultaneously *rise* to your divine destiny. *Rejuvenation* occurs as we navigate through the maze in which opposition in all things are interlaced within the blueprint of our life path. Rooted and open to the expansion of duality and its *rejuvenation,* we are afforded the opportunity to learn how to take command within the dualities of life. We learn as we are curious over what is reflected to us.

Stepping onto the dance floor is an example of how we can gain insight to working with the principle of opposition. As we take to the dance floor with our partner, we can exchange places and learn from another perspective and then, learn that there is another perspective and many more. Hence, the gift of opposition! Just as with strengthening a muscle, we provide resistance for the muscle to have to push up against it; over time with consistent practice and effort, our muscle develops strength and size. In turn, we do the same thing with *rejuvenating* our muscles. We test our stamina in making choices, owning them and seeking to align with our purpose. To do so, we must have opposition.

Opposition is necessary, and life offers various kinds that test us. Some opposition comes in the guise of temptations to go against our committed course. Some are mortal challenges we feel are thrown on us. Some come at a high cost, and some are a mere bump in the road, yet no one is exempt. As we persevere, we will be led to the other side and gain peace from the storm. This peace may require the price of learning and growing to become refined through the very hard stuff, heartbreaking moments, and challenging choices, surpassing the temptation to quit, and enduring to the end.

Now you may ask, what does endure to the end mean anyway? It simply means living your truth. As you battle through the minutia of the duality and nonduality and become acquainted with your Ideal Self, you will be in tune with knowing what you brought with you through the veil of forgetfulness. In addition, learning from this inner healer what lessons you are to take from your past trauma and how to maneuver through the carnage to *rejuvenate and* regenerate to becoming a new you. Your Ideal Self is waiting Inside you, anticipating her release to jump out and up in truth and openness, freeing you from expectations and definitions which no longer serve you. Your PTSD has caused you to be someone different than who you really are, stuck in your armor of the pseudo-self. It's time to shed the lie. It's time to live your truth and embrace your life.

Now, step up and out from your PTSD and observe. What is needed at this moment to get a grip? What is inside that really wants to be talked about and expressed? What is your truth? And what is needed to reach out and show up for the love of your life? We are not meant to live on an island alone in this world. Your marriage is your purpose, and it too can be *rejuvenated* along the way. Begin by making the decision to embrace your truth now.

The truth of the soul is your power.

One of the best ways to find contact with our sense of purpose is via meditation. As you bring your awareness to your Sacral Chakra and the energy that resides here, imaging becoming one with the Creator, the power of duality become evident. Bring your inner energy to this Chakra, and let it show you how you would see the world through its paradigm. Feel your body, feel your intuitive guidance, and go with the flow. Focus on opening the energy in the sacral Chakra and experiencing the sweetness of creation, noting how it ignites the heart and stimulates you.

You will find there are a variety of ways we can stimulate the mind, body, and heart as your nurture and nourish your intuition specifically for getting to know you. This is the key to opening the way to connecting with duality, receiving its gifted reflection of your non-duality self, opening the way to *rejuvenating* toward your Ideal Self, and freeing you from the bondage of your past trauma.

While you continue to focus on your Sacral Chakra, inquire and ask the burning questions that percolate to the surface and ponder on them. Some thoughts you may be curious about could include: What is it that you want to leave behind? What is it that you know in your heart no longer serves you? And is *now* the best time to release it and allow yourself to *rejuvenate*?

Remember, you are in communion with your inner healer, your co-creator manifesting as your Ideal Self. Intention is yours to own; embrace its power to eradicate the distorted thoughts and beliefs which no longer serve you. You have arrived at this moment as it's time to create new space for an expanded life as you dreamed. As you take charge and live your intention, you connect to your creative power and show up as your Ideal Self; this in turn is the determining factor for raising the quality of relationships to others.

If damaged from past traumas and unattended to, the *Sacral Chakra* is often activated by fear, and you are vulnerable to becoming preoccupied with power dynamics, external influences, and attachments. Choices become a struggle. Your struggles manifest in battling with poor social skills, frigidity and rigidity, fears of intimacy and change, lack of desire and passion, or losing all motivation, to name a few.

Since the developmental stage for evolving into one on one relationships occurs between six and twenty-four months of age, these insecurities have been with you for a long time. During stressful times, you are vulnerable to feeling challenged by your emotional identity. How to feel may be lost if there is a disruption or trauma during these months of development.

Yet simply by knowing this, you can now tune in to the Sacral Chakra envisioning it and begin to feel it – be with it. The healing begins with self-gratitude. As you place attention to your feelings and identify what you want and feel, compassion to yourself can create a relationship with yourself that opens the door to start one with another. Developing balance in the sacral Chakra requires building trust and having faith that the commitment to healing will be supported by your inner knowing, your Ideal Self. You can begin to do this by exploring your fears and their causes and letting them breathe. Then counter anything that comes up against your inner truths whispered from within. As your emotions show up, let them flow, feel them and let them go; emotions are energy in motion. Remember, the Sacral Chakra loves all things creative and artistic: music, poetry, painting, creative writing, architecture, or DIY crafts. Investing time and energy to express who you are through these mediums will cement who you are from beyond time and space, taking you far and above any PTSD, so you are no longer defined by these past experiences.

When we are stuck in our trauma states, we unknowingly are managed by the lack of internal resolution that sits at the pit of our stomach. The broken story becomes your narrative of defensiveness, fear, and finger-pointing in our most intimate relationship when you could be cradled in the arms of your lover.

As you engage in conflict in which you are projecting your energies and story on your partner, the reaction of anger, shame, and guilt is sent your way. This is a hook to staying engaged and venting out similar feelings back to your partner that can be justifiably exonerating. However, this does not lead you any closer to your dream come true.

When the culprit to your imprisonment of despair and resentment and self-loathing is your PTSD, your partner is not the bad guy, and neither are you. In fact, your partner is your best friend in this scenario, as he is mirroring back the reflection of your PTSD shadow that hovers over you and now your marriage.

While stepping back and looking at your relationship from this perspective, you can create a paradigm shift of taking the wind out of the battle immediately. Now don't get me wrong, we all have disagreements, and confrontations are an integral part of relationships. Yet when contention is a byproduct of being hindered by the shackles of PTSD, you and your partner are not on the same team.

As you begin to look at yourself more than your partner, you will come to discover and uncover truth and learn that you are the author behind every accusation. The concerns expressed toward him are reflections of yourself you have yet to recognize or accept. As the internal resolutions occur, your responses will sync in harmony with your partner, rather than angry judgment; you will express curiosity, understanding, and openness. Yin Yang is a great analogy for a marriage. The diagram provided by Tao Te Ching offers a good visual *Yin Yang* symbol for greater clarity. To see a color illustration, download the free companion PDF to this book at aplace2turn.com.

Two halves, you and your partner, complete and whole. Yin and yang are also the starting point for change. There is wholeness, all is complete and unchanged. And when you split the whole into two pieces – yin and yang – it upsets the equilibrium of wholeness. In turn, wife and husband end up chasing after each other as they seek a new balance. Again, the dance of duality and nonduality is in action. Reflecting on this symbol reminds us that the law of opposition occurs in all dyads, including, marriages as well. This concept is recognized as a critical part of the marriage, the ebb and flow of the yin and yang dance; therefore, PTSD cannot trip upon the continuous movement in the steps of duality and nonduality. The unity of dancing produces the marriage. In other words, the PTSD is now viewed as an opposition they band together against in walking in the storm of tribulations; know this too shall pass, and the dual will be stronger for it. Lastly, the yin and yang symbolism remind us that neither you nor your husband are complete in the marriage without one another. You are interdependent upon each other as you require him and he requires you to be present to be married. And at the same time, the nature of husband and wife flows and changes with time and can be dramatic and transforming.

Knowing that transformation occurs in duality and non-duality, you can then place your attention on enjoying the journey as you do your own personal healing and simultaneously celebrate your marital evolvement to becoming as one.

Transformation opens the way to remembering and *rejuvenating* what was forgotten (through the veil) and joining this knowledge with the experiences – good or bad – with day to day life. This puts you in your creator mode and master of making your dreams come true.

In my work with couples, I have grown attached to Don Miguel Ruis' *Four Agreements,* as I find them to be a workable template to launch from resistance with opposition toward the greater eternal perspective.

His first agreement is being impeccable with your word, meaning being truthful and following the truth from within. Self-betrayal occurs when you allow any thought or behavior into you being that works against you, detouring you from your truth. Hence, being impeccable is the opposite. When you are impeccable, you are accountable for your responsibilities, and you do not judge or blame yourself. So, when you're impeccable, your word counts, and you don't use it against yourself.

While, embracing your truth behind your intention to show up living your purpose, the other three agreements offer *rejuvenation*. They encourage you to avoid taking things personally or assuming you know the story and then to do your best, simply manifesting a relationship free of any divisiveness based on fears that accumulate from refusing to show up.

Doing your best is good enough, and it's the fuel to charge the inner engine to act. Remember personal power is not taken; you either give it away or abandon it by allowing outside forces to make your decisions. Knowing differently is the key to getting a grip of your PTSD as holding a pebble in the palm of your hand. As you embrace your power, important shifts in self-awareness and insight occur that break the PTSD chains that have anchored you to the victimization archetype, until now.

As you are in the process of *rejuvenation*, upon reflection, you may look at the reflection mirrored back to you in this world of duality and still see a fracture pictured of you as your Ideal Self. Fortunately, all the pieces are here, and with the decision made to *re-awake* and stand strong, you can witness the miraculous dance between duality and non-duality which makes *you,* and thus the *rejuvenation* has just begun. As you continue to evolve through *The Triangle of Mastery*, your mirror will reflect your growth from the ugly duckling mired in PTSD into the magnificent swan you contract to show up for your journey ahead.

When it comes to PTSD, forgiveness comes in phases along with the healing of the trauma itself. Forgiveness is a key element in the healing process and necessary for it to be complete. Your relationship with forgiveness directly impacts your spirit as unresolved hurt impacts the essence of who you are, and the pain ties you to those who harmed you. Forgiveness is letting go of this toxic connection. It's about you taking a stand and making the choice to release all ties that hold you hostage to being defined by the past.

I address forgiveness at this juncture intentionally, as you are not meant to do it alone. This is an opportunity to build on the trust you are establishing in your key relationships now by sharing your story and decision to forgive your partner. This lets him know you are needing him and have made the choice to love him versus nurturing the wounds from the past. A simple exercise of sharing what you need to forgive with specificity is a major step toward freeing you from the bondage and preventing personal vulnerability. You are present and showing up! By uncovering the past lies, their power over you and the attached shame dissipates, and now the wounds can heal. This is your opportunity to renounce the deceit that held you hostage and take back your power to create the life you desire. As the pain disperses, your inner healer can enlighten you with the truth that has always been. Ask and listen for the whispering from within to reveal it. Reflect and integrate this truth, notice, and imagine life living in it. Empowered with your truth, doors open to then share your Ideal Self with your partner as together you witness powerful changes from here on out.

To see a color illustration of *The Triangle of Mastery's Step 2: Rejuvenation,* download the free companion PDF to this book at aplace2turn.com.

Chapter Seven

Real-I-zation of the *I Am* Creation

"One thing: you have to walk and create the way by your walking; you will not find a ready-made path. It is not so cheap, to reach to the ultimate realization of truth. You will have to create the path by walking yourself; the path is not ready-made, lying there and waiting for you. It is just like the sky: the birds fly, but they don't leave any footprints. You cannot follow them; there are no footprints left behind."

— Osho

W hat does *getting a grip on your PTSD* have to do with *real-I-zation*? In order to know your Self, you need to know where you start. *Real-I-zation* is the step of getting to know who you are so you can know to where to start being and becoming your Ideal Self.

Recent studies indicate that trauma may very much be part of our entire life from pre-conception to the present, coined as developmental trauma. Adverse Childhood Experiences Study (ACE Study) has conducted research that has demonstrated a correlation of adverse childhood experiences or trauma with health and social issues throughout our lives. Their study expands between 1995 and 1997 with long-term follow-up for outcomes. It was conducted by the American Health Maintenance Organization Kaiser Permanente and the Centers for Disease Control and Prevention. The results included substance misuse; physical, sexual, emotional abuse; physical and emotional neglect; intimate partner violence; mother treated violently; substance misuse within household; household mental illness; parental separation or divorce; and incarcerated household member. The negative effects of ACEs are felt throughout and affect individuals across all cultures. The Substance Abuse and Mental Health Services Administration (SAMHSA) provides a pyramid diagram with a nice visual picture of how failing to treat PTSD may impact and interfere with evolving into the Ideal Self where love and joy resides.

To see a color illustration, download the free companion PDF to this book at aplace2turn.com.

As can be seen, an awareness of how developmental PTSD impacts *are* defining you. The time to know who you are is now and begin to build your path toward the Ideal Self.

The third step, *real-I-zation*, invites you to choose to be Self-aware versus defaulting to auto-pilot and coasting through life. As we engage in the present moment and stay *awake*, we can step out of the trance of reacting to whatever life throws at us. Rather, we can observe, take ownership in your part of the activity occurring, make a proactive choice as how to participate, and emerge with authenticity and wonder as you were made to be. The challenge is to be ready to be real so your *I am* can surface and *rise* to *be*-ing the sensation you were born to be.

As you are actively involved with every step you take, you can capture the silver lining to every cloud that comes with the trauma. As previously shared, opposition in all things is a law of necessity in order to grow. When trials hit, you are faced with the *re-awakening* to remembering who you really are in mind, body, and spirit. Recognizing that you are an eternal being, change is more readily welcomed, and knowing is an aspect of progression toward the Ideal Self. I liken this remembering to your subconscious imprinting what you entered life with, including the cellular data pasted down via your DNA from multi-generations so that as you step out of the past and embrace the present *as is*, you begin to untether from the ramifications of your trauma.

You begin by grasping this moment and do the work to *rejuvenate* in mind, body, and spirit. And to do so you must first know your enemy and make the commitment to yourself to get a grip!

Making a commitment is a stamped promise to your Ideal Self who, again, carries the memory beyond the veil of forgetfulness and directly communicates with God. Therefore, these steps place a superimposed auric triangle over *The Triangle of Mastery,* representing a three-way covenant for your success between your-pseudo-self, your Ideal Self, and your Creator.

This idea can remind you that you are not alone, as this three-way covenant can be your mastermind team. Just as Napoleon Hill shared in his book *Think and Grow Rich*, by engaging in his creative imagination, he developed his own support team as he laid in bed at night before going to sleep and invited the mentors of his choice to this round table, then made himself available to learn from them. In this creative process, Napoleon Hill evolved and manifested into the man he desired, as well as the husband his wife adored. While he wrote his book, he simultaneously kept a journal, which was published in 2012 as the book *Outwitting the Devil.*

This journal contained all his traumatic experiences life dealt him throughout the thirty years of getting *Think and Grow Rich* published. He states he needed to walk through his own challenges to learn this very lesson of getting out of his own way in order to master the very concepts he outlined from his research for *Think and Grow Rich*. Humbly, he openly shares his human way of getting a grip on his own traumas. Not only did he meet his earthly ambition to write and publish his book, he transformed and became the master of his own soul.

He metamorphized from caterpillar to butterfly.

Knowing you are not alone and choosing to use your knowledge of having a team covering your back, the freedom that awaits you can *be* and together you are ready to get to work.

Everyone to one degree or another experiences developmental trauma. Unfortunately, many individuals have also struggled through societal, war, persecutory, and many other traumas.

Fortunately, more and more research is occurring and developing insights on how PTSD impacts you. ACE is the most extensive research conducted that shows the impact on the individual as to how you think and act. Studies are enlightening us regarding the impact of untreated PTSD and how it interferes with the ability to process fully from your physical, mental, emotional, and spiritual selves. ACE studies show how trauma retards the organic neuropaths of the brain, resulting in blocking access to your own metamorphotic experiences and the intuitive knowing and ability to trust and act in every way. The most frightening aspect of this is all this can occur without any awareness at all.

Our world has set you up with all the conveniences of *not* having to engage with your intuitive abilities. We can create a whole person by putting meaning and definition to the projections from the outside in. We have all kinds of props and assistance to do so at our very fingertips.

This comes from others' hidden agendas – much a by-product of their unresolved broken stories media and artificial intelligence and all the evolving *magic* Artificial Intelligence has to offer. The outside stimulation can clog our brains with so much noise and chaos. How can we not be on constant overload, overwhelmed emotionally and downright fatigued? Unfortunately, there is not a lot of emphasis on taking the time to learn from within where your Master Healer can truly walk you through the mirage of chaos to the oasis of peace. This cocooning process begins here.

The third Chakra is where you hold your personal power. The Solar Chakra is located at the solar plexus, the home where your personal power resides. It is said that the role of your third Chakra, known as *Manipura,* is to translate vision into reality. Its meaning in Sanskit is *the palace of jewels*, as it gifts you the ability to transform dreams into meaningful treasures, teaching you the insight of coming to understand how you are able to dream your desired world into being. The center of your body, physical and auric, can be the starting line where your dreams alchemically turn into gold. The solar plexus is centered in your body having access to the grounding benefits of being rooted to Mother Earth and nurtured by finer energies of empathy, joy, and faith. As a result, you – the *I am* you are – are literally rocked back and forth in the eternal arms of Heavenly Mother and Father to whatever degree you allow for this to *be*. As you can imagine, experiencing this love and compassion from your Creator and the whisperings of hope and faith in your ear, you can *real-I-ze* your *I am*. Why is this important? What does this all mean? Again, by starting where you are and choosing to show up for yourself, embracing the memory, your own intuition gives you your accountability partner. As you take charge and act on the empowerment gifted to you, you are able to conquer your past fears and shed your trauma! You may question how this can be this easy. All I can say to this is out of small things, great things occur.

As you evolve into the Ideal Self, you are able to hear, see, and walk through the veil where you come to know that your life course is already imprinted on the subconscious and conscious and can better understand the purpose behind all that has occurred. This does include the marvelous and wonderful things in life, as well as the trials and hardships. The intuition is never not there, whether you choose to ignore it or not. It is always available to you and designed to be at your beck and call.

Trauma takes you off your mark and then continues to haunt you with its chaos and noise, as its major teaching objective is to capture your autonomy by teaching you that what you think and feel is wrong. This takes you hostage by paralysis, fight or flight mode, all to keep you from the present. You then become hampered in showing up and taking action according to your highest and best self and left with merely coping – let alone breathing – therefore trapping you into the outside-in learning matrix and sacrificing your connection from the inside-out learning.

Where to begin? First, seek the quiet so that you can return to your natural sense of connecting to your primal part from within. Then focus your attention inward as it is through your body that intuition is felt. These physical sensations let you know your intuition is communicating with you. Remember the times you experienced chills running up and down your limbs and spine or the knot in the pit of your stomach, bursting into tears out of seemingly nowhere, and that overall sense of just knowing.

It is my challenge to you to set this book down for a few moments and practice embracing your intuition now by doing the following:

1. Get in a comfortable position so that your body can relax; breathe in the fresh, clean air, and as you exhale, let go of all that is unnecessary now.

2. Next, simply notice how you feel this moment as you turn your focus inward and to your solar

plexus. Ask from your center core what it wants you to know, and listen, paying attention to the sensations experienced as your intuition speak through images, sensations, sounds, fragrances, or words.

3. While this is transpiring, seek to locate where the messages live in your body, mind, and/or spirit to gain the intended insight into their meaning.

4. Next, and most importantly, be willing to surrender and let go of all resistance in hearing and seeing all that you may have been missing

5. Lastly, journal your self-hypnotic experience. Again, you are your own best teacher, and logging the new insights as they come can offer additional lessons and wisdom down the road.

This is it; now, take the challenge beyond this experiment and make it your daily practice.

It bears repeating that your intuition communicates with both sides of the veil. Your inner healer picks upon more than your thinking brain. As you integrate a consistent practice, it becomes a routine in your day to day life so that even when you may not be in the mood or simply do not want to, you will know that by surrendering to the magnificent gift that is a part of you, you can know all that you need to know. You come to *real-I-ze* you know more than you know you know. In the end, listening to your whisperings from within will guide you toward breaking from the entanglements of past trauma and lead you to the life you are meant to live.

This Solar Chakra is said to correspond to your developmental stage in life of adolescence, between ages of fourteen and twenty-one, chronologically. It is key to our blossoming and maturing into adulthood. Without a strong sense of *real-I-zation*, you may not be functioning at your highest and best and may indeed be failing in your desired endeavors. Even with all the resources for success at hand, you may have found yourself lacking the stamina to get to the finish line, as you have run out of steam. When sidelined by negative experiences and unresolved brokenness, or if used destructively, your *I am* is repressed. This in turn hinders your primary nature, or libido, and manifests as neurotic symptoms of shame or guilt. Another way trauma can impact your *I am* is compensation or creating a coping mechanism of inflating ego and often seeking to control others through intimidation. This makes you vulnerable to falling into the delusion that you are the sole author of your destiny and can subject the world to your will. Now the best way to regain perspective when or if you experience any feeling of disconnect for your sense of self is to lose yourself in the service of others. It may be time to take a step back and revisit the duality in your life. You may have disconnected from your key relationship and need to re-align the yin yang dynamic. This can also be addressed by serving those around you now; by interacting and working with others, you are gifted a mirrored reflection of how where you are or are not showing up now in this life. This provides information that can give the ability to get back on track.

The Solar Chakra is your luminous energy system, your power center. It's the power that fuels your journey toward manifesting your aspirations in the world as it employs the fulfillment of our dreams. When you *awaken* to the *real-I-zation* of your power, fearlessness and resolve will run through your veins, and you will not be deterred by adversity and obstacles that seek to crumble your world.

The *I am* center is your truth and the expression of your own nature. Your life purpose becomes clear, and you are aligned with it beginning from within and into reality.

Seeds to *real-I-zation* are gratitude and appreciation. When you choose to live in a state of gratitude and appreciation for your life, you send this signal to the Universe that you have everything that you need to meet the purpose of your life – hence, desire. This in turn will attract needed insight, creativity, and hope into your life; then by application of these attractions, you come to see how the world is a reflection of you. Adding more to the previous challenge you took advantage of doing and recording in your journal, you can now apply these steps to everything that comes your way to bridge the gulf between the experience and your ability to see how it's part of your purpose. Again, as the main character of your story, you can ask:

1. Where are you? Who are you with? What are you doing? What can you see, smell, hear, taste and touch? Focus on the sensations and feelings and make them as real as possible.

2. Imagine – create the identity of who your desire to be and witness the transformation; how would you act? How would you talk? How would you walk, think, feel, dress and make decisions? Act *as if* you until it becomes your natural state of being.

3. Clean up the weeds, that is, your clutter – let go of the old to make room for the new to bloom in your life. Let go of anything that no longer serves you or does not help you to feel your best.

4. Prepare for your dreams to arrive by truly expecting your dreams to occur. Ask, what would you be doing to prepare? Do that now.

5. Ask for divine guidance – Seek God's will and key into your Ideal Self; then listen for the whisperings from within to know right where you belong. Surrender control and begin to pray and ask for daily guidance to move you in the direction of your goals and dreams.

6. Let go of attachment to outcomes. There are an infinite number of ways your desires can manifest in your life; cultivate an open mind and an unwavering sense of trust in the unfolding of your dreams.

7. Follow your intuition, trust in your *I am* guidance, and take action on it. When it comes to manifesting your dreams, you can do it!

8. Feel good now – be happy now *as* you create your dream-come-true life.

9. Live in the present moment. If you are constantly reliving the past or worrying about the future, you will literally miss out on seeing and experiencing the beauty, blessings, and miracles all around you. Touch base with the present moment by noticing the sights, sounds, and smells around you.

10. Journal – Write, observe, and witness your journey. Describe in great detail as it unfolds and how happy and grateful it makes you feel.

11. Celebrate *you* and your evolution on your eternal trek.

12. Affirm within – Feel it and be it to assist the reprograming of your subconscious to stay on course in manifesting your *I am* and *real-I-zing* all that you can make happen. Want it to happen, and you can make it happen! You are the star of your show.

13. Put effort and consistent practice in your creative imagination. It's one of the most powerful ways for you to show up and engage your Ideal Self. *Re-awaken* and *rejuvenate* to *real-I-ze* your imagination by being curious and asking yourself questions such as: What is the most outrageously,

amazingly awesome thing that could happen to me today? What would I love to happen today? How can I give to the world today?

14. Find ways to live today – Begin by showing up; key in to your luminous center to power up your dreams. If you dream of becoming whole, you will. If you dream to love and be loved again, you will. If you dream to be all that you can be as the wife of your spouse's desires, you will.

All of your actions create new feelings and vibrations inside of you, and as you choose, you will in turn attract opportunities for the fulfilment of your dreams. To see a color illustration of *The Triangle of Mastery's Step 3: Real-I-zation,* download the free companion PDF to this book at aplace2turn.com

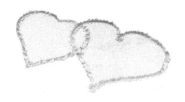

Chapter Eight:

Renew your Heartfelt Magic

"There is no difficulty that enough love will not conquer: no disease that love will not heal: no door that enough love will not open... It makes no difference how deep set the trouble: how hopeless the outlook: how muddled the tangle: how great the mistake. A sufficient realization of love will dissolve it all. If only you could love enough you would be the happiest and most powerful being in the world..."
— Emmet Fox

The heart is the area where physical and spiritual meet. It is the heart Chakra which covers the center of the chest and includes the heart, cardiac plexus, thymus gland, lungs, breasts, and rules the lymphatic system. The Sanskrit word for this Chakra is *Anahata,* which means *unstuck* or *unhurt.* In other words, beneath the broken stories and unresolved grief and pain lies a well of unquenchable wealth of love and joy, home to the Ideal Self and inner healing resources. For me, the heart represents a pure and spiritual place, the healing home where no existing hurt exists.

The word *Anahata* is associated with air in reference to the elements God used in creating the earth we call home. Each power center interrelates and integrates with one another as do the elements harmonize to give life energy to sustaining our home.

The Root Chakra is *re-awakened* through the earth to providing steadiness and groundedness. The Sacral Chakra of *rejuvenation* represents water as it brings forth fertile creativity; the Solar Chakra, home of *real-I-zation,* is the fire in the belly as your transformation into *I am* brings your grounded creativity into action. Now the heart disperses the energy of power, like the air we breathe oxygenates and integrates spiritual understanding, love, compassion, and joy everywhere. Love, like air, is within and all around.

As you open your heart, you become *renewed* and filled with flowing love and joy from within. Healing comes in an instant, not so unlike the magic that occurs when you experience love at first sight. Without notice, Cupid's arrow strikes your heart, and instantly, the fireworks ignite the electricity from within, opening your capacity to join in oneness with another.

This power of love of anahata *renews* the heart. The significance of this is that it addresses the other side of the coin, forgiveness. The *renewing* process consists of being in a place to consciously and deliberately release feelings of resentment or vengeance toward a person, situation, or group who played a part in subjecting you to your past trauma. This is regardless of whether they actually deserve your forgiveness; instead it is forging your way toward evolving to living an unconditional loving life for yourself and another.

Over the years, clients would express concern about forgiveness, as they feared that by doing so their perpetrator would walk away as if no wrongdoing ever occurred. Yet forgiveness does not mean forgetting, nor does it mean condoning or excusing offenses.

When we work from the insight of an eternal perspective, we are reminded that we do not have the power to walk free from a misdeed because our victim forgives us. They too are completely different animals, as I will demonstrate in the forthcoming story of Wild Bill. In her book *Profound Healing*, Cheryl Canfield shares the power of the forgiveness and love of the man known as Wild Bill.

He was an attorney who was also a Polish Jew during WWII. The Germans came to his neighborhood and yanked everyone from their homes, lined them up, and executed everyone.

Wild Bill was preserved because of his profession and his ability to speak five languages, including German. He witnessed his wife and five children executed before his eyes.

Despite the rage that tore within him, he shared that he knew what hate did to the men's minds and decided right then and there to love every person he came into contact with whether he lived a few minutes or years more. Despite serving six years in the same concentration camps as everyone else, he walked out in the same condition physically, emotionally, mentally, and spiritually as when he entered.

He did as he committed, he rooted, rebounded, and *rose* to love all. His love kept him whole, and his ability to love went hand in hand with his decision to forgive. He knew that holding any attachment to the horrific acts of the soldiers toward his family would not add to the condemnation for them; it would only hold him hostage to hate and prevent him from showing up to live the life God persevered him to live. By choosing to live now and pressing forward with a purpose to love, he grew to serve and inspire many on becoming whole.

As can be seen with Wild Bill, as he chose to be in a place to be quick to forgive and love, he mastered the

7 Steps of Root, Rebound, and Rise, living a life of the triangle of mastery as his blueprint in life.

On the other hand, those who hold onto their fractured hearts are unable to *renew,* as they can give way to unresolved grief, self-betrayal, fears, and even hatred. As trauma creates a case for choosing to remain in a place of grievances, the hurts turn to scars, defining them you by their past.

Living in the past trauma keeps the emotional brain on high alert, as if the danger is still present. This puts the Pseudo-Self into action, who can only react to what life brings you. Reactivity tosses you into the throes of fight/flight and freeze mode. As the belief grows that only more of the same is possible, you are re-creating the patterns of past over and over.

Unlike Wild Bill, it may appear that there is no other way to experience life after trauma. You may feel you would be stupid to be anything but on the defense. After all, if hurt once, the shame goes to the perpetrator, yet if you don't put up a defensive stance and you get hurt again, shame on you, right? But you get to choose what to do with your hurt. You might choose revenge; being lost in the confusion of fear of the darkness from the pain you experienced and accumulated hatred. Yet, that is not living from the unquenchable well of love and joy but rather a closed heart.

When encountering pain from your past or present, you have a choice on how to feel them with the intent to then let them go or choose to hold onto them. By living in the now, you are more likely able to let them go and open your heart for *renewed* love for people and experiences with compassion, charity, and understanding. On the other hand, harboring hurt creates negative feelings and shuts out loving feelings and opportunities to be present and *rise* to your highest and best expression to serve as your desired now. Although it may feel counterintuitive – as your mind and your ego may tell you – when coming from a place of feeling so broken, letting go is a viable choice. By making this choice to let go, you are freeing yourself to move on.

You ask how to make this happen. Wild Bill became famous for the loving service he showed to others in the camp and beyond, and he was made whole.

Serving others *renews* our heart, and our heart offers a *renewing* of those we serve. As we come from the heart, we can walk in the shoes of another, experiencing life through their perspective and developing a sense of empathy that becomes the healing balm for your pain. Now this may seem impossible for you to do, yet if you engage your creative imagination and ask, "What if that person…?", you are able to explore possible scenarios of the complexity of their life stories. By creating a host of scenarios, you can realize there are endless possibilities and one for which you can begin to extend empathy and compassion toward the other person. This can take you away from your pain and begin the process of resolution as you hold compassion for another. Now, you may say it's different from someone who is repeatedly hurt, who has a pattern of inflicting pain and betrayal, victimizing from a cold-hearted place. Yet you can still offer love and compassion from a distance or by setting boundaries. You now ask "Why?" Why should you care to offer those who hurt you or another anything, let alone send energy of love and compassion?

As you come from your heart center, you are reminded of the rewards of self-compassion and the freedom from being attached to the wrongdoing of others. When someone hurts you, it's never about you, and it's always about them. And you want to keep it that way.

The wrong doer who remains a wrongdoer lives a life patterned after the pseudo-self only. They work at creating a motive in telling a particular story or anecdote which supports a stance of no culpability or blame. Hidden agendas are a communication pattern that nurture wounds and aid in not forgetting the stories behind their broken heartedness. If you choose to stay attached to the dance of righting their wrong from the past, you fall privy to the games of manipulation and deceit that causes *stuckedness* in your growth. Unfortunately, the self-serving motive behind your hidden agenda fertilizes the *not forgetting* and blossoms into unforgiveness and trapping you into taking on your perpetrator's story – becoming prisoner, shackled with hurts which belong to the perpetrator.

When making decisions, you may assume you are your brain, and you may well be; however, you may also involve your heart. Culturally, we have been conditioned to use our brains for everything, forgetting our heart has more magnetic energy than the brain itself. According to the Heart Math Institute, "the heart's magnetic field, which is the strongest rhythmic field produced by the human body, not only envelops every cell of the body but also extends out in all directions into the space around us. The heart's magnetic field can be measured several feet away from the body by sensitive magnetometers. Research conducted at HMI suggests the heart's field is an important carrier of information." Every dis-ease begins with imbalance in the body's energy field and, more specifically, with how your heart interacts with your brain and body. Bringing balance to your system begins with *renewing* your loving power from within by the fears and dissonance, which, make up all possible dis-ease. With the heart producing an electrical field 100 times greater than the brain and a magnetic field 5,000 times greater, the heart could be considered the center of our intelligence. Hence, *the heart wants what the heart wants*. The power of our heart introduces our conscious awareness of active and dormant energies. It acts as a bridge for all the Chakra points or power centers to resource from and re-ignite the flow of consciousness and unearth the inner healer to mend the fractures of your broken-ness. Again, this is accomplished by the meditative appreciation exercise from the musical frequency of the heart rhythm as I participated in at Heart Math training.

As we expand on this in chapters ahead, you will come to understand the magnitude of change that this one exercise can produce with consistent practice and effort as being a key in all the tools, exercises, and insights of each of the *7 Steps to Root, Rebound, and Rise*. Every heartbreaking memory carries an energy that is counter to moving forward. As you practice the meditation at the end of this chapter, you can learn to turn the energy back around with the healing power of gratitude. Then, your fears can be eradicated, breaking the grip of your PTSD. Just as the cobra sheds its dead skin to grow, you too can grow as you shed your limiting beliefs and thoughts and replace them with appreciative energy toward living in a strong and heart-centered way. As this is achieved, you can embrace self-compassion and kindness and prioritize showing up in your intimate connections again. By choosing to feel, think, and speak from your heart, you *renew* the love power in all your interactions with life. As you choose to listen from within, with the intention wrapped in love, you become aware of the synchronicities that occur within your life story. Some call this divine timing; others deny so, as there is no interest in experiencing life from a *renewed* perspective and, at the most, call it luck. Your emotions are vibrations of energy which influence your reality, and as you choose to *renew* your perspective of coming from the heart, this becomes the source of energy that offers balance to your emotional state and physical wellbeing. The two emotions from the heart are fear and love, and only one of them can reside in the heart at a time. It is also said that all the other emotions are varieties of these two. When fear and the emotions derived from it consume you, it creates a blocking of energy pathways for progressing forward. Fear inhibits all capacity of *renewing* possibilities by inhibiting creativity, blocking manifestations from your intuition, and resulting in the breakdown of our immune system.

Love and the positive beliefs and emotions derived from it have a high vibration that is expanding; hence, it enhances creativity, builds physical and mental endurance, increased productivity, and high perspective. As can be seen, the quality of energy field you create within your heart has a direct impact on influencing your experience and reality. As you come to understand this *renewal* process of listening how the heart sends out its own signal to the body and brain, the responses are back in accordance to the healing elements that occur under the spell of love.

And when you add trauma into the picture, this communication breaks down. Fear enters the heart, and you fall back into the fight/flight/freeze reactions and/or rational thinking is countered with feelings of being numb/apathetic/ indifferent and shutting down the flow and hindering your ability to choose how to act. As the heart dominates the two-way communication, its complexity has its own admirable qualities, and by diverting your energies back to the heart, gratitude is discovered in lessons learned and the fear is replaced with love once again.

Knowledge is power, and as you come to appreciate your own power of love, you begin one step at a time to *renewing* from within your heart center and drinking from the unquenchable well of love and joy. The meditation exercise that I learned from the Heart Center is as follows:

Simply begin by placing your hand over your heart, and imagine speaking directly from the heart when you encounter another. Simultaneously acknowledge the gratitude you experience by choosing appreciation from within. This is the first step in *renewing* your marital covenant; choose to feel and experience it from within your heart, and let the behaviors follow. Trust the process, as it may feel counterintuitive to your brain. Evaluate what you desire to create in yourself and in your relationship. Step back and re-evaluate your life situation thus far. Stop and take a moment to feel the celebration that arises in your heart when you are choosing to express your love and joy, and then act according to the celebratory thoughts that follow. This is where the appetite to show up, give back, and create a difference toward *renewing* occurs. Build on these steps by making it a routine and consistently practice to envision your happiness and joy. During this exercise you may add reflecting on your marriage as you want it to be and then finish with overall gratitude for being the *you* who is clear of fear and illusion of hopelessness, committed to rising on forward. I want to add one more vital yet small healing gesture; when all seems too hard, smile again. A simple smile can trigger those happy hormones and calm the nervous system and slow the trauma reactions down in order to regroup and get you back on track more quickly and easily than you may anticipate. Remembering life is a journey and as you grow to see challenges as finetuning for your desires to manifest fully, you will naturally begin to foster love and loving feelings, undeterred by any storms that may pop up along the way.

As you are now more aligned with your Ideal Self, in sync with your heart, you are ready to *renew* your marital bond and spark the passion that has gone dormant. I say dormant, as energy is never lost. We are eternal intelligences and energy. As you embrace your energy of love and then share it, you link your biochemistry and behaviors with your spouse. This in turn creates the magnetism of *like attracts like* and an underlying motive to invest in one another's well-being that brings *renewed* hope for changing and getting back on track in re-igniting the passion from within your union again. This interactive dance creates a positive resonance, a reverberation of love energy that is self-sustaining and ever-growing into a lasting bond that can endure the good and the bad from this day forward. Learning that love is a renewable resource, together you and your spouse can forge ahead, no longer fearing the ground is going to cave under you. This well of love and joy shared back and forth will serve as a deep and abiding sense of safety and security from the storms of the past and those that may come ahead. As science is now showing that trauma is stored in the cells of your body, then from a body's perspective love is positivity resonance and provides nutrient-rich bursts of energy that accrue and become building blocks for healthy and happy bonding. In truth, the body hungers for a sense of oneness, and this feeling arises when you and your spouse *sync up*. This shows itself as you two literally act as one, finish one another's sentences, and move in rhythm of the same beat – biologically you are on the same wavelength, connecting in mind, body, and spirit.

Knowing the true power of love, you will discover loving behaviors naturally following as each of you reach out to one another for a hug, sharing inspiring and humorous times, finding peace in silence, and leaning on one another's shoulders in difficult times. These nonverbal gestures of oneness forecast a bonding appreciation of connecting. With consistent practice of *renewing,* you will generate the eternal bliss that once was only dreamed about, and together you will be directed toward health, happiness, and both being your Ideal Selves where intimacy can tie you together and offer a mutual sense of trust. In turn, within this intimacy bond, your love continually flows, even in the most unlikely moments, transforming predicaments so you can stay present in action and reinforce the safety of your bond. Together, you enter the race to hold on to the marriage built on the trust and openness of your *renewed* hearts of everlasting love and connection. John Gottman, a leading scientific expert on emotions within marriage, suggests that couples who *bank* their shared positive emotions can use them to help get through later tough times. In his research, Gottman discovered that couples who use and store up positivity resonance are more equipped to navigate the emotional upsets that can be threatening to their union.

To see a color illustration of *The Triangle of Mastery's Step 4:Renew,* download the free companion PDF to this book at aplace2turn.com.

Chapter Nine

Revive and Reinvent Yourself through Innovation

"A further sign of health is that we don't become undone by fear and trembling, but we take it as a message that it's time to stop struggling and look directly at what's threatening us."
— Pena Chadron

O nce you take a stand, know your place, show up, and give of your heart, you are ready to speak up by *reviving* the vibrational sounds of your voice. As you open your mouth and voice your truth, you claim your power of choice. Your free will is the greatest gift from above. The Throat Chakra is known as *Vishuddha* in Sanskrit, as it references the first of the three spiritual Chakras within you. This region governs the throat area and all that is used to speak. Its power source encourages you to speak up, listen, and express your Ideal Self, where faith and understanding govern your language and intention. The element for the Throat Chakra is space, or ether, as well as a sense of hearing.

Reviving your power to voice in expressing your authenticity and choice can be a challenging task, especially if your free will has been trampled on from your trauma. Knowing that you have established a strong foundation by mastering the first four steps, you are now ready to show up, state your choice, and speak your truth. This is now accessible. *Awakening* puts you at the starting gate standing tall; while *rejuvenating* offers lessons of accountability to show up and overcome the fear of entering the game of *your* life. *Real-I-zation* endows you with your personal power and the integration of your Ideal Self infused with the confidence to *be* present and opens the way for the *renewing* of your heart so that now you can *revive* your voice and verbalize your needs and desires that mirror the truth of your Ideal Self.

Once you claim your voice, you want to state your truth. Dr. David Simon, who was a world-renowned authority in the field of mind-body medicine, co-founded and assumed the role of medical director of the Chopra

Center for Wellbeing where he offered three gateways to bridge the gulf from your trauma state to speaking your truth and free will. He suggested you first inquire within yourself, "if what you are about to say is true." If so, then ask, "Is what I am about to say necessary?" And if yes, the final gateway is, "Is what I am going to say kind?" As you can see, this is a simple formula. Yet it can work to ensure you have not lost sight of your Ideal Self and you remain impeccable with your word. Thus, you are free to speak your highest truth as your truth is the voice of your spiritual essence manifested through kindheartedness and compassion.

Words are important to take notice of as they matter in that they are energy and have their own vibration like every other aspect of life. As a result, what and how you express yourself does reflect on how and who you are showing up as. Positive affirmations are a great first step in expressing a desired intention for increasing your vibration for connecting with likeminded people. However, my clients have shared frustration in getting their energy to shift into higher gear and to buying into the belief of the affirmations they are spewing out. Their struggle is a by-product of their failure to begin where they are at versus where they wish to be or think they are. Hence, they show up for the wrong race from the get-go. Again, you must first know yourself, then know where you are at the start of the race. First, begin by affirming and validating the current emotional state.

The struggle occurs when you are carrying around incongruent feelings within and reinforcing the *stuck-edness*. As a result, you are left with either being muted from expressing your desired choices or inadvertently living a lie. Don Miguel Ruiz, author of *The Four Agreements,* developed a formula for communication that ensures speaking from a place of love and power versus fear. His first agreement is to be impeccable with your word. Honesty begins from within. The tendency to formulate our words to how we want to be perceived and even manipulate the outcome is a common trap of delusion and grandiose self-loathing that traps you into the performance played by the pseudo-self and the "outside-in" circus, entertaining the world by chasing your tail. If you want to get off this merry-go-round and begin to move forward in living your life of truth, you start with having mercy for yourself right where you are at *now*. You stop and make the choice to take the action step of putting the oxygen mask over your face and breathe the breath of life into your soul.

Another trauma *stuckedness* is a form of blocking out the Ideal Self where you don't show up in life except in a reactive role of the pseudo-self, and you only matter as someone's punching bag or acquiescing to another's will. Someone once shared that if she was on a private jet with only herself and the pilot and the oxygen mask dropped, she would give her mask to the pilot, completely oblivious to the fact he has his own mask. She lacked any awareness of herself, unable to conceptualize the celebratory experience of self-love and the evolution it offers.

How do you get unblocked and open the air pathways to bringing life to your soul? You begin where you are at and then take one step at a time. You validate each baby step, acknowledging the honesty and truth for where you are at as you look forward to the adventure ahead. Hand in hand with speaking up is listening. Listening is another aspect of *reviving* your purpose. The Ideal Self listens with the capacity to giving the other person your full attention. This empathic gift is the very glue to the marital communication that synchronizes the verbal and nonverbal dialogue with your marital partner. The phrases "reading each other's mind" and "finishing one another's sentences" occur when your intention is to see through your partner's eyes and share the very air he breathes. This opens and broadens the paradigm possibilities of seeing the world and the dual awareness of knowing you are not your trauma. One of the greatest deceptions I witness is where the client creates a paradigm attached to their trauma, i.e. "I am an adult child of an alcoholic" for themselves. On the surface, yes, if your parent(s) is/are alcoholics, you are a child of an alcoholic, yet this situation is not *you*. Attaching yourself to a label from the outside in creates a vulnerability to bonding under the umbrella of your wounds, another face of *woundology*.

Marrying with the bond of *woundology* keeps your PTSD in the middle of your bed and this dominating influence shades every interaction between the two of you. In turn, you are shielded from one another's light and unable to wrap your arms around the barrier of the rusted armor created by the pseudo-self for protection. This is a condition that haunts many marriages where trauma is a visitor. Blinded by the pseudo-self where reacting is the only mechanism for healing, running from the relationship seems to be a logical avenue to find safety. Thus, divorce has become the most common fracturing and divisive choice of your culture and a paradigm that offers one lens, not *the* lens to observe and live life. As you successfully evolve through your *real-I-zation* step, your options and opportunities expand on acquiring infinite lenses to witness life through to capturing lessons. Learn to develop your Ideal Self and how to conquer your trauma without fracturing your life, your purpose and loving union. The more successful you are with this adventure, the greater ability you have to stay unattached to outside paradigms and agendas that rob you from your Ideal Self; therefore, remaining free from the noose of your past traumas and free to live and love your mate for life and eternity.

Sound is one of the most powerful healing vibrational energies we have to use. *Aum* is the vibration of God and all His manifestations. It is all matter, all energy, and all thought. It's a reminder that all things were by Him. Its interpretations include, Amen; Holy Ghost; Amin and Hum. Sound is said to encompass three vibratory energies required to create, preserve, and destroy.

Laughter is another way to raise our energy via our voice. My mentor Zarathustra introduced me to his method of active meditation. As a self-professed hyperactive individual, he found quiet mindfulness contrary to his auric energy field and discovered active meditation more calming and healing within his journey of *reviving* him to meet his calling.

Zarathustra taught me the power of my own laughter and introduced me to a journey of allowing my childlike nature to shift my perception in matter of moments. By engaging in the belly laughter of a child, an innocence of wonder opens up and a surge of energy zaps you *awaken,* and your reverberating pulses of electricity runs through your body. It's as if I drank from the fountain of youth. You can actually feel an internal tickle that percolates into giggles, and you make a connection to your Ideal Self and the joy filled heart of another. The contagious laughter is a magical way of shifting your paradigms in unison to see that most things in life are not that important. Your two hearts meld into an open trust and with an added humor that can remind you that sometimes the offbeat ways are the clearest path back to re-discovering one another.

Laughter allows you to step outside your space- and time-bound state and touch the field of awareness that is boundless and eternal. The place where memory resides, and purpose is stored in its purest form and brightly lit as a neon sign, is to not be missed. As the quote from The American theologian Reinhold Niebuhr summarizes for us, "Humor is a prelude to faith and laughter, and is the beginning of prayer."

From the perspective of mitigating your PTSD, laughter works elegantly as a mind-body phenomenon that reduces the production of stress hormones and boosts the immune system. In turn, your humor can decrease anxiety, soften anger, lighten depression, and increase your pain tolerance. This *is* getting a grip of your PTSD, as your happy hormones and chemistry clear the neuropaths of your brain like clearing scar tissue away from the wound, opening the way for the mind, body, and spirit to communicate freely and openly bathing you in the *now* perspective of the rest of your life.

From the experience of my own laughter, I have allowed myself to be carried away in the ether of *now*, and I encourage you to do the same. Then take your spouse by the hand and bring him with you to share a life of humor, laughing out loud together, tickling one another's funny bones, and lighten up! Be creative and give yourself permission to commit acts of silliness and lightheartedness.

Vocal expressions of gratitude for the choices you make is another form of *reviving* you to your potential. You can create a gratitude list as you did for the heart communication.

My gratitude-for-the-choices-I-make list, looks like this:

- My choice serves me by providing me with a sense of security because...
- My choice serves me because it acts as insulation from all the unwanted energies around me.
- My choice serves me because it makes me overcome my fears and insecurities.

This is just a snippet. Your list can be – and I encourage it to be – ongoing and endless.

Now, words, positive affirming intentions, sounds, laughter, and gratitude are a few things you can do to create a safe space for your inner self to become fully self-expressed. As you engage in these exercises, you will discover new convictions percolating, especially as you look into the emotions, past traumas, and even current situations and relationships that no longer serve you.

I believe that the more you apply these exercises to your daily routine, the more you will experience the energetic, mental, and emotional root cause to all the pathologies of your PTSD and be able to eradicate the toxic hold it has on you. You will come to discover how these simple modalities become part of your methods of creating ineffable spiritual experiences into your daily life.

Now that you know that it is far simpler and more fun than you had imagined, you can embrace the opportunity.

You are the creator and shaper of your destiny by the choices which you voice. You *rise* and fall in exact accordance with the character of the choices you entertain. Your environment is the result of what you create as you engage free will, and your circumstances in the future can be shaped and built by these present desires, aspirations, thoughts, and actions. You choose and pursue empowering choices by consciously building the destiny that will *revive* your free will and successfully align with your Ideal Self. Here, your wisdom can be beautifully expressed as your voice breathes the spirit of a calm and authentic mind. The vibrational tone will correspond and ring with a grateful melody that soothes and inspires. This, in turn, will resonate your true heartfelt nature and touch the soul of your loved one healing and expanding you as a couple. I hope you can see now how this cocooning process is truly creating the butterfly that you are. You make or unmake yourself. If you encase your desires in the armory of the rusted metal, forging forward with weapons in hands, you will continue to sabotage your true intention.

In turn, as you override the abuse and wrong application of words from the past trauma and no longer accept being enslaved by the confinement of the pseudo-self, you will remember that you are the maker and master of your destiny. Then stop and take note of your will's intent and conviction. You will become the butterfly destined to fly the path of your voice and choice and arrive at your heavenly mansions of joy and strength and peace, ascending you to your Divine Perfection.

To see a color illustration of *The Triangle of Mastery's Step 5: Revive,* download the free companion PDF to this book at aplace2turn.com.

Chapter Ten:

Restore the Intuition Within You

"Thoughts become things. If you see it in your mind, you will hold it in your hand."
— Bob Proctor

The 6th step *restore* corresponds with the Third Eye Chakra, which is associated with the element of light. Now that you are empowered with the first 5 steps, *Re-awaken, Rejuvenation, Real-I-zation, Renew, and Revive*, you are ready to re-align fully with your Ideal Self and rejoice in the *restorative* nature of feeling whole again. This enlightening experience occurs as your purpose solidifies into a vision both temporally and spiritually, illuminating everything as it is without the filter of your past, your expectations, or your judgment. The Third Eye Chakra is located at the third eye, which is between and just above your eyes, presiding over your visual perception. In Sanskrit, this power center is called *Ajna*, meaning command.

In other words, it means taking control of your life in the *now* and illuminating everything filtered from your past, your expectation, and your judgement. As your vibrational energy *rises* to the third eye, your connection to higher knowledge, the subtler aspects of sight and intuition are *restored*. With *Ajna* Chakra *restored,* you can begin to see things as they are from an eternal perspective, rather than colored by expectation, projection, and ego. As you see more clearly, you are freed from your past trauma's darkness casting its influence over your light preventing your ability to see all that there is to see. From there, you see what you want to see. The Third Eye Chakra is associated to the pineal gland. Our pineal gland is in the center of the brain and is the center of attention due to its relationship with the perception and effect of light and altered or *mystical* states of consciousness. It's also associated with regulating your biorhythms of sleep and wake time, including your dream world. The pineal may well be the gland that has the highest concentration of energy in the whole body due to its makeup, which includes being bathed in highly charged cerebrospinal fluid (CSF) with more blood flow per cubic volume than any other organ. It is no accident that it carries so much responsibility in aiding you to be able to see all there is for you to see.

The Third Eye Chakra magically *restores* vision, intuition, perception of subtle dimensions, and energy movement, clairvoyance and clairaudience, access to mystical states, illumination, connection to wisdom, insight, inspiration, and creativity. As you see who you really have come to *be* now, you *awaken* your third eye and *restore* your intuitive sensibility and inner perception.

What does all this mean in regard to getting a grip on your PTSD and saving your marriage? As you focus your mind and consciousness, this light allows you to see beyond your PTSD and have the insight to *rise* above to create a deep alignment with your Ideal Self and *restore* your marriage.

The marriage *restoration* is freed from the entanglements of *stuckedness* of the past, the delusions of fantasies of what *could have been*, being blinded by the pseudo-self, rejecting the spiritual aspect of the union, or being blinded from the greater picture due to the foggy vision. The ability to *be* present in mind, body, and spirit as your Ideal Self and within the marriage of your dreams requires faith as a key ingredient in the process of seeing the unseen. Faith is the fastest means toward transcending here, as it is this discerning eye that sees beyond the veil and opens us to wisdoms of the eternities. And this concept must be practiced, like strengthening the muscles in our body. So, it's no surprise that faith without works is dead. This faith is a spiritual gift, yet one we all have. If you are finding yourself feeling no faith, all it means is you are currently conditioned by your tribe or environment; the worst-case scenario is your faith is dormant… You are not without it.

You create faith by visualizing and believing in attainment of your deepest desire. This state of mind can be induced by affirming your deepest desires until your subconscious believes your will and this becomes the emotion of faith. In his book *Think and Grow Rich*, author Napoleon Hill places faith as his second step toward attaining achievement. He states faith is belief and asserts that in order for you to accomplish anything in life, you must first have faith (believe) that it will happen first.

This spiritual gift of faith offers a quickness in your observation that is an antecedent to and is linked with another spiritual gift of discernment. Discernment is the light of *restoration* which protects and directs in a world that had grown increasingly dark and opens the way out of this black tunnel. The light is the miracle. You can see how faith precedes the miracle. Hence, as you become quick to observe in the name of faith, you then come to know you are prepared for this gift of discernment. Then by discovering its light, you are provided its protection and direction to seeing all that you want to see. The power of discernment's light exposes the shadows of the wrongs done to you as you gain an acute sensitivity to impressions – spiritual impressions, if you will – seeing under the surface, detecting hidden evil, and in the end, finding the good that may be concealed. The highest type of discernment is that which perceives in others and uncovers for them their better natures, the good inherent within them. Hence, as you embrace this discernment you can see the dual nature of your past trauma, and this leads to detaching from the PTSD, as well as, discerning the spirit which influences you. As you have already made the choice to show up as our Ideal Self, you can more successfully detect falsehood and mean intent from the truth and love. This opens the way to allowing the love for and from another into your heart, prompting joy in your thoughts and coming to know you. Once you know you, you can know who you are within the marriage and how to make it to become what only dreams are made of.

As you stand up for your burning desire to love your husband happily ever after, it will be backed by your faith. This faith becomes your external elixir of life, power, and action to the impulse of your third eye vision. Napoleon Hill, author of *Think and Grow Rich*, states that the emotion of faith is what gives "life, power, and action to the impulse of thought." He states this happens as you transmute your major defined purpose into physical reality, and for this to happen, you must have faith, belief, and be convinced that you will accomplish this. As you accomplish your purpose, you can see the goal of a happy marriage already achieved before its materialized in the real world. This act creates the feelings of faith, and your mind becomes as you were created in Self and union.

As you build on this pattern of faith, you come to remember how its human nature to see what we want to see and ignore the rest. If your expectations come from within and above, you live a life of *restoration*.

There are variety of assertions of the premise that we see what we want to see, as K VanLehn's Repair Theory claims that there is a tendency to read a written sentence and miss the errors, so he developed techniques, which determined how our brains will read the sentences as though they were written correctly, and not see the typos right in front of our face. H. Hill & A Johnston's 2007 article, *The hollow-face illusion: Object-specific knowledge, general assumptions or properties of the stimulus?* In Perception, 36 (2), 199-223 DOI: 10.1068/p5523 shares another theory, the *hollow mask* experiment that demonstrates by rotating a Charlie Chaplin mask it show how we perceive the hollow surface of the mask having a nose. This protruding image is based on our expectation and prior knowledge of a normal face that has a protruding nose. Consequently, we subconsciously reconstruct the hollow face into a normal face. Their results found ninety percent of what we see gets lost by the time it reaches our brain. The finite nature of the brain leaves it to a guessing game of missed information based on experience, in which you can find yourself stagnant and stuck within the PTSD matrix.

Other neurochemicals, including pinoline and DMT, are metabolized by the pineal gland that connect the mind, body, and spirit. More specifically, melatonin quiets the body and mind, opening access to the higher consciousness while pinoline and DMT are psychoactive and impact perception, mood, consciousness, cognition, and behavior.

All this explains the fascination and curiosity with the association of enlightenment and immortality to this pinecone shaped gland. Spiritual traditions credit the pineal with symbolizing growth and the unifying force that underlies creation and opening the third eye of inner vision, insight, and wisdom. Pinoline enables visions and dreams in the conscious mind. While DMT is found to be produced during deep meditation, giving birth, sexual ecstasy, extreme physical stress, and near-death experiences, it's also been found to alter dream consciousness upon its release into the bloodstream during the Rapid Eye Movement phase of sleep. DMT-induced visionary experiences and non-ordinary states of transcendent consciousness link the body and spirit. The activated pineal gland also influences our experiences through vibration rhythm. This offers healing through sound.

Rhythm entrainment, or resonance, happens when the hypothalamus and pituitary entrain with the pulsing vibration of the pineal gland, shifting our whole system toward harmony.

Besides being sensitive to light and vibration, the pineal gland is also activated by exposure to magnetic fields. Like when the heart is activated with the high frequencies of love and compassion, its electromagnetic field is amplified and expanded. The pineal gland's sensitivity to electromagnetic energy causes it to begin vibrating and activating in concert with the heart. As these two organs entrain together, their high vibration opens the third eye to greater inspiration, intuition, and inner vision. And lastly, as the pineal gland has a connection with spatial orientation and circadian rhythms, it shifts perception of space and time when it is in a highly aroused state to expanding the consciousness.

As this is a lot of information, and much that may require you to look further into the scientific background to more fully understand, my intention is to emphasize the miraculous elements of healing you have with you and how every sense has more intelligence than you may know to tap into that offers endless, literally endless, means to become whole.

Prana or breath work is a great place to begin at each step, yet I place extra attention with restoring your vision and knowledge as oxygen feeds the brain and reaches every other level along the way. The Nadi Shodhana Pranayama is the breathing technique that reaches the energy channels run throughout the body known as nadis, which transports the prana into every cell of the body. The energy channels are connected to the subtle body versus the physical body, bathing and *restoring* your spirit with the energy to *rise*. This technique focuses on three channels: ida, pingala and shushumna nadis. The shushumna nadi runs parallel to the spine while the ida and pingala nadis wrap around the staff, which looks like a DNA double-helix. As the nadis spiral up the spine they cross paths at each of the seven Chakras and then all three intersect at the third eye center, restoring the intuition and knowledge. This exercise entails plugging one nostril and taking a few deep breaths out of the opposite nostril. Then, plug the second nostril and do the same. This practice is designed with the ultimate goal of creating balance by clearing any blocks throughout the system that are inhibiting your ability to *restore* and then *rise*.

Tapping is the exercise from the Emotional Focused Therapy (EFT) that you can use anytime to *awaken* the meridian centers in the body by tapping. As you gently tap your forehead in between your eyebrows, the vibration sends a wave directly back to the pineal gland, activating it in the process.

Another way to wake up and restore your sight on the mark is through active meditation. Smiling opens both the heart and the crown, allowing more light to penetrate while also increasing the vibration of the organs. Laughing and smiling reduce stress and relax the body, which increases the flow of chi. Laughter also triggers the release of endorphins, promoting feelings of well-being. Relaxation increases blood flow, which amplifies the effects of the hormones and has an effect of pineal gland activation.

All these simple exercises can take you to a higher consciousness as it is during our altered states that we break through the illusion of time and space, where you can better address matters in the present and resolve the unfinished business that occurs during trauma.

Trauma is just that – stories that were beyond our understanding, which hurt and then are left unresolved. As you are able to create an ending of the story, you are able to grasp the lesson that can be learned and forgive what at one time was unforgivable.

There are many ways to enter an altered state. We do it all the time; again, we fail to recognize our own healing tools from the inside out. Human evolution has provided advances beyond many an imagination, yet in that process, mankind has seemingly discarded the most valid and timeless healing from the inside out. Fortunately, they are not extinct; they are safely stored within our being, preserved by your inner healer. As you re-align with your Ideal Self, you become re-connected with your inner healing and happiness, and joys are at your fingertips.

Once you have the vision of your Ideal Self and the path of your *restoration*, you can then turn your focus toward restoring your marriage. Again, you must attend to your unfinished business before you can show up for your spouse and then be present with him. The perspective of the sixth step is from above the clouds giving you the ability to see beyond the horizon of the story of where you started. As you have explored the unseen for yourself and evolved into your Ideal Self, you can now do within your dyad. As your intuitive sense witnesses where you start and end and then where your spouse starts and ends, you can then meet him where he is at. As your third eye is *awakened*, you have the insight to see life through your partner's eyes and beyond. The knowledge from this higher perspective opens the way to stand where he stands, root with mutual convictions and accountability, walk his walk and define the dance for moving forward, celebrate the individuality of one another and the diversity it has to offer for creative evolution, love from the intelligence of the heart with Christ's consciousness, speak a mutual language honoring free agency, and see beyond the past, be in love, and journey forward hand in hand. The connection begins, and your journey together is on to *restore* what once was lost and now is found.

To see a color illustration of *The Triangle of Mastery's Step 6: Restore,* download the free companion PDF to this book at aplace2turn.com.

Chapter Eleven:

Resurrect Your Sacred Contract

"You're looking for three things, generally, in a person: intelligence, energy, and integrity. And if they don't have the last one, don't even bother with the first two. Everyone has the intelligence and energy – you wouldn't be here otherwise. But the integrity is up to you. You weren't born with it; you can't learn it in school."
— Warren Buffet

The Crown Chakra, *Sahaswara*, is itself the energy center of *renewal* and transcendence, hence the *resurrection* of your Ideal Self in full bloom, symbolic of the thousand-petal lotus flower. This power center is also associated with *Om,* the sound of the Absolute. Representative of all that was, is, and will be – the center of creation. This step of evolution is the peace of being above and beyond any trauma from the past, residing in incomprehensible purity, *renewal* and beauty and tying you to the Divine. Here, your Ideal Self integrates with your Creator for enlightenment and spiritual connection that reaches beyond and throughout the eternities. This opens you to the *real-I-zation* that you are in the realm of pure awareness and consciousness. It is here you come to know all you are meant to learn from the good and the bad, with all of its surprising twists and turns that direct you to your purpose in its purity.

Arriving at step seven, *resurrecting* means you have successfully maneuvered through *The Triangle of Mastery,* transcending through all the fears and barriers that prevented you from freeing yourself from the past. This trek toward your freedom and ability to *be* in the now opens your vision to the previous unseen wisdom, which translates you to your highest state of consciousness. Now as your spiritual energy is most dominate, your burning desire to engage in progression toward the future of infinite possibilities leads to memories of your knowing more than you have known you know. Again, we are reminded of Albert Einstein's quote that "once a mind is expanded, it cannot contract." This applies to the spiritual and actualized energies of the subtle mind that are connected to the intelligence when we entered this earthly dwelling. As you *resurrect*, time and space no longer limit you from knowing all you are past, present, and the future. This expansion offers a grander picture of all that occurs in this earthly realm. This greater perspective is truth and it is truth that sets you free.

Once you've established a daily practice of these activities that connect you to your Ideal Self and the Divine, you will see expansion of spiritual awareness in your marriage. You will begin to experience unconditional love on a consistent basis, that taps into your inner healer bathed in the balm of eternal perspective. You will be more compassionate, kind, and forgiving, and you will show more humility. Life will no longer be solely about you and your desires. Your life will become more about serving your partner, as it is about loving all those with whom you come into contact. You will have your own Wild Bill heart's desire, knowing as you serve him you are healing and loving yourself and mending the marriage.

In a twinkling of an eye, Wild Bill knew where he stood, his relationship with mankind, *real-I-zed* his healing came from the inside out, embraced the healing power of love, chose how to *be*, envisioned his Ideal Self, and then manifested his Divine purpose and meaning in his search in life. Wild Bill keyed into the *why* as his guiding light to stay on course as he understood that the way to survive all suffering is to love, work and maintain his dignity. Nietzsche's words ring so true here, "He who has a why to live for can bear with almost any how."

The PTSD's mantra is rooted in *I have nothing to expect from life anymore*. Yet even if you believe in this lie, you don't need to expect anything from life. As we evolve into the butterfly and view life from an eternal perspective, we *understand how it does not really matter what we expect from life but rather what life expects from us.* In the illuminating light from above, we anxiously engage in taking responsibility to discovering the answers for the challenges of life and fulfilling the tasks set in front of us.

Ask yourself, are you staying true to what life expects from you? Have you sought to remember your purpose? Have you taken accountability for choosing life? Have you welcomed the messages reflected back to you about you as messages of where you start so you can know how to begin? Have you sought to know yourself and *real-I-ze* you are you for a reason beyond this world? Have you dived in, opened your fractured heart, freely loved as it is the only way to heal the brokenness? Have you found your voice and moved forward with speaking up in determination to spread your purpose? Have you befriended your intuition and high knowledge to go where you are called to go? Now can you stop, take a breath, and embrace this newfound freedom of your *resurrected* state? Can you allow your Ideal Self to shine through in all her brilliance and gift you a life

To Love... & Beyond where the grip of your PTSD has loosened, and the ramifications are no longer? You may not be where you want to be in life right now, and you do see the bigger picture. You are standing tall with a clean slate and open hearing so that you are now prepared to join in common with your partner in your committed destiny to build a happily ever after marriage. The avenue of getting there is unique to your union, incomparable to any other marriage.

Free from the tethering of your past trauma, you can focus on the salvation of your marriage through the love and being in love process. Victor Frankl was another causality of the concentration camps in WWII. As a psychiatrist, he had developed his theory, logotherapy, of overcoming all PTSD through love. Unfortunately, Victor Frankl was taken to the concentration camp before being able to present his manuscript for professional consideration yet put it to practice as he was forced to endure the camps for the next three years. He engaged his creative imagination and remembered the love he had for his wife. Despite being married, he had been separated from his wife as she was sent to a female camp while he was sent to the male camp. Despite the deprivation and horrific conditions, Frankl found salvation in the love that he had for his wife as he embraced a perspective from the inside out.

I imagine that if I could sit and hear his story, I would learn that his journey would be *The Triangle of*

Mastery's 7 Steps to Root, Rebound, and Rise evolution. He rooted in standing his ground by knowing where he started; he had a ticket to America to present his work, yet he could not leave his family behind during the war. He understood the dual pull of who he and who another was and *rejuvenation* as he built on the common connection and the foundation of the love all are born from. His *rea-I-zation* of his autonomy gave him the insight on how he wanted to show up even in the darkest of times. With his *renewed* strength of these foundational steps, standing tall, he gave from his heart filled from the healer from within. This provided the reciprocal stamina to *revive* his voice and be undeterred by the outside storm. Instead, he recovered and *restored* his sight on the vision of his truth. Living his truth, he opened his awareness to the wisdom greater than himself. And in the end, he *resurrected* from that concentration camp to become whole again. Real or not, his imagination and living from his inspiration of hope and eye on the eternities, he was able to live the power of love. Love was an antidote to the pain he endured during those years and achieved the desired fulfilment and meaning in his life. He remained unscathed by the outside world as nothing could touch the strength of his love, thoughts, and the image of his purpose to love.

In addition, Victor Frankl states he learned that the human body is tougher than you think as he witnessed in the camps the extraordinary amount of punishment that the human body is capable of resisting, giving another testament of the resilience from trauma and ability to heal your original state of being. The spiritual freedom regarding behavior and reaction to any given surroundings is the key to *resurrecting* from the imprisoned effects adversity. Frankl argues that this is proof that you are not bound to any environment you find yourself in. Despite the harsh determiner to any action you take, it is not fate, as you always have a choice. As you accept accountability for your life and fly above to create choice of action, you *can* preserve a vestige of spiritual freedom, of independence, of the Ideal Self, and you literally will *resurrect* and be untouched, even by the most dire and terrible conditions of psychic and physical stress.

As your PTSD experiences have shown you, you may not have had a choice in your circumstances and environment. But you can see as you choose to *Root, Rebound, and Rise* you are empowered with the wisdom and strength to act and know how to react to all that is imposed upon you.

The path of *The Mastery of Triangle* does not seek to completely eradicate PTSD from your life, as, following the law of opposition in all things, happiness cannot be had without its opposite. So the goal of getting grip of your PTSD is to discover the meaning it can have on your life.

This is a good place to revisit the law of opposition. To resurrect we first root, then rebound from the good, bad, and indifferent in life along the way to *rise*. Each step along the journey is where we define the experiences into lessons to learn and grow. One of the most common questions asked from the sufferings of PTSD is, why does there have to be suffering? To answer in the context of *To Love... & Beyond* paradigm, beyond the low of opposition in all things, there must be meaning in suffering. Suffering is an ineradicable part of life. Suffering and happiness are needed for human life to be complete. In the end, your Ideal Self chooses to designate meaningfulness in greater ways so to create ample opportunity for added deeper meaning in life built on moral values to sustain the most difficult and build a thriving marriage.

Your Ideal Self recognizes from the inside out that life overall is an opportunity and a challenge. Every experience has its victory and can turn a trial into an inner triumph, hence finding meaning that will keep your life, including your marriage, full of purpose and joy. Seeing from the illumination of the *resurrected* Ideal Self, you come to know the close connection between your state of mind – your courage and hope or lack of them – and the state of immunity of your body will understand that the sudden loss of hope and courage can lead to the demise of all joy and life of you and your marriage.

Louise Hayes shares in her book *Heal Your Body*, "If we are willing to do the mental work, almost anything can be healed." Her book came about from her personal experiences of loss and trauma, and she learned that there is no coincidence that terminally ill patients with strong convictions have a greater chance of surviving. Their illuminated perspective of hope, meaning, and a belief in a future of meaning and purpose can save you from your own illness and resurrecting you to your sense of purpose.

Life is the period between one breath and the next; the person who only half breathes only half lives. He who breathes correctly acquires control of the whole being. Imagine bringing the cleansing energy of an exhalation and then *reawakening* with the energy of an inhalation, surrendering, and honoring your natural rhythms. Imagine arriving at the completion of a circle of life, in which deep healing and *rejuvenating* is occurring in your mind, body, and spirit. Imagine experiencing your *renewed* Self as you have discarded all the dead parts of yourself today.

You are your own Healer – the true healer in all instances. You are your best teacher as we see what we want to see, we hear what we want to hear, and we come to know what we want to know. Being one in heart with your Maker is the prototype for life and especially for your marriage. As you define who you are in this *resurrected* state, you are at the starting gate of the race, showing up to win the love of your life back.

In the end, how does this translate into having a happily ever after marriage? As you evolve through *The Triangle of Mastery* and work each of the *7 Steps to Root, Rebound, and Rise*, metamorphosing from a caterpillar to a butterfly, momentum building and transformation beginning to move out of the trauma cycle and into joy, love, and wholeness. As you gain understanding and meaning of all that happens in life, you transcend the suffering and enjoy the fruits of God's law of opposites in all things. The fulfillment of being is achieved as your Ideal Self *resurrects* to embrace your husband in your arms of unconditional love and strength to transform together free from your rusted armor to fly to new heights, making your dreams come true throughout the eternities.

Harmony and unity necessitate the understanding of your spouse. This leads to developing an infinite understanding with seeing more and more clearly the internal relations of things and the eternal purpose of experiences of life. As your Ideal Self, you have come to govern yourself and know how to adapt to others, and they, in turn, reverence you as they witness your spiritual strength, and learn to rely upon you. Hence, a marriage is reborn. In this *resurrected* state, your tranquility transmutes to greater success, influence, and power for good. You will find your husband drawn to your equable demeanor, loving, and revering you. Tranquility and serenity resonate from your union, and, together create a life of truth, beyond the storms for eternal harmony and joy.

In the core of your soul resides your Ideal Self who carries the divine love and joy for true and complete healing. As you *resurrect* her and allow her to show up in your relationship, you are in partnership with your Creator who helps maintain your relationship contract. The triangle of mastery is complete as three eternal intelligences join forces as one, beginning with the couple reaching up to the heavens and being showered by the healing heart from above the triangle that looks up and follows which are greater than one.

To see a color illustration of *The Triangle of Mastery's Step 7: Resurrection,* download the free companion PDF to this book at aplace2turn.com.

Chapter Twelve:

Rise and Refine Fear and Obstacles

"Misfortune — and disease — is simply an imbalance in the natural harmony. It occurs when we're alienated from the wisdom of the invisible world, when we're trapped in limiting and disempowering stories about our lives."
— Dr. Alberto Villoldo, Grow a New Body

I ronically, as you travel through *The Triangle of Mastery's 7 steps of Root, Rebound, and Rise*, it becomes clear that consciousness (spirit) generates matter (mind and body). In other words, everything is spiritual before its temporal. So what happens between matter and spirit that bridges them together? What Is the transforming element? Quantum Theory asserts that the wacky behavior of our atoms – photons, electrons, and the other particles – dance together to create matter. Then we have the thinking realm where James Allen teaches in his book *As A Man Thinketh* the power or energy of thought determines emotion. We also have *Quantum Healing* by Depok Chopra who demonstrates how one's thoughts and emotions can lead to mysterious and wonderful healings of the body that are only describable as miraculous.

So, what is the conclusion?

My answer is it's a mastermind endeavor. What these theories and many others have in common is that there is a relational dance between creative forces. Energy and intelligence manifests into life force, engaged in a grand journey of building that transcends space and time, moving from the micro level to the macro level of life. As you come to understand the complexities of your reality, you are left with the awe of the marvelous work and wonder and can appreciate there is so much more to life than how it appears or can be seen from our earthly story.

If you accept this vision, you can begin to live life in a completely revolutionary way! Lying just beneath your everyday perspective is a truth that is amazing beyond your imagination.

One of the greatest fears I hear from my clients is having no control of their destination. As they believe life happens to them and the cards are not dealt in their favor, they become paralyzed. Fear becomes the emotion that mentors them, nurturing the startled response of the fight, flight, freeze reactions to cope. As these responses of our emotional brain are only meant to be built-in mechanisms to get our attention to address imminent danger and not meant as proactive measures for moving forward, we can get stalled by misusing them as tools to evolve.

When stalled, it is common to reflect on what was or what should have been as means to rationalize the need to react and stay put. Unfortunately, the longer we stay there, the harder it is to see ahead. As we get lost in the darkness of the past, we become consumed with the fears and pulled under like walking through quicksand. This illusion becomes real as our thoughts and emotions materialize in our day to day life. Life begins to be hard and painful. It can seem impossible to move forward, and we find ourselves stuck in the muck and sucked under from cycling through the past traumas and living ramifications that are now destroying the marriage. When all seems lost, you have a hard time looking forward and seeing any future, let alone a positive one. This distorted perspective creates a belief that you live a life of toxicity and/or the world is a hostile place. Helplessness can take over, and learning to manage it seems to be all there is in life. It can feel like, look like, and then be like life is happening to you and you have no control, ability, or say in what comes your way. You are stuck in the developmental stage of fighting to survive and finding you are not one of the fittest. Life may not even feel worth living anymore. It's hard to want to take another breath when all you inhale is blue butane from the fire-breathing dragon of fear.

Clients have shared they cannot imagine life happening for them nor believe that all or any thing works together for their ultimate good. You too may perceive life as if its happening to you; hence, the challenge here is to start seeing it all as happening for you.

Quantum energy demonstrates this to be the case as the universe itself, down to its most basic elements, has to have been spiritually built to fulfill our every conscious and subconscious desire, belief, thought. Hence, the mechanics behind our healing is beyond this earthly realm. We are created to love from the intellect of beyond. As you fight to *rise* from rooting and rebounding through the 7 Steps of your *Triangle of Mastery*, you will begin to see the possibility and the truth behind these building blocks, beyond space and time, and actually hear, see, and know you. This is your Ideal Self who has been patiently waiting for you to show up and *rise* so you can hear, see, and know more than you can stand up and be your heart's desires.

No doubt, reading and learning of *The Triangle of Mastery* didn't immediately squelch your fears nor ignite fireworks within your being at first sight. Yet, it is magical, and it will change your life. As you make the choice now and take on the ICAN attitude, you will walk through the fiery fears, let go of any remaining armor of inhibitions that hold you back, and find your way to rooting, rebounding, and *rising*. These 7 Steps will lead you across the seen and unseen gaps that work like showers of loving essence, where your thirst will be quenched from the fountain of joy discovered within you and your hunger filled with faith that brings courage and strength for the journey ahead.

These quantum gaps are the bridges that connect you to your Ideal Self, and it is she who carries the loving wisdom that will reunite you with your husband. Then together, you can begin to learn the parallel walk where you travel hand in hand moving forward.

Just like the conscious thought process encounters breaks and blank spots (another form of quantum gap), your relationship interaction and dialogue may have encountered the same blips that escape awareness the moment it occurs; when this happens there is a tendency to go on automatic pilot to fill in the unknown with whatever old conditioning you carry in its place. This ends up looking like you are back to square one and all of this is a facade. And it is, unless you make sure it is not.

Each step is a learning process, not unlike learning to ride a bike. As for me, it took me literally two years to ride a bike. I could have easily quit; I felt alone and had to battle my imbalance, as it was up to me to get over the gap for fear that interfered with staying on course. This did not only take eighteen to twenty-three months longer than my sibling or friends; it brought along with it many a scraped knee and dozens of band aids. If I had stopped getting on that bike and keeping my focus forward, believing and holding onto my desire to ride, I would not have mastered the balance needed. I would have developed the belief I was too clumsy and needed to accept my lot in life. Fortunately for me, I stuck it out, I did not let the scars on my knees dictate defeat, nor did I harbor anger over the seemingly impossible feat before me. Between the ages of five and seven, I gained a vision between the seen and unseen. I had the faith that my heart's desire was met, and I only had to keep stepping up and forward, and I would come to see its fruition. I may not have understood what the driving force behind my perseverance was, yet I was able to act on it and the result manifested. At that time, my Ideal Self led the way, and my pseudo-self could not shadow her. I seemed to know as I just breathed through each experience, all was good enough, as I could breathe through the next and the next until I reached my destination. The unseen is the subtle energies that are part of our journey. As balls of energy we can increase our vibration until we see the unseen. Our energy field's colocan be seen, altered, and rebooted, as energy is the creative force of manifesting all that is – what it is what we create. We can gain an understanding of this and seek to make life happen, or we can be human robots and live as if life is happening and exert very little energy and live a cycle of *stuckedness*.

Unless you stop, breathe, and learn to take notice and embrace your energy states of the quantum gaps of the unseen you will keep re-creating the same story over and over. This is the scariest thought in my book. A scraped knee can heal, just as Victor Frankl healed from his most horrific life trauma. As long as we have breath we can heal and evolve and live a life of unquenchable abundance of love and joy.

It is my theory that you are here – right where you are at *now* – for a purpose, and I encourage you to stop and observe all that you perceive at this moment. Then breathe and take note of your insights, vision, and inspirations that percolate from within and thread the tapestry of your blueprint and roadmap toward your purpose. Now, as you a ready to act, flow, and sing the ICAN mantra, as you will naturally progress forward in your eternal journey.

The greatest fear we face is the unknown. This is the most common reaction I hear from clients at the thought of change. What is the unknown? It's a lot of things: It's the fear of failure or criticism. What if you *rise* only to find yourself in a worse situation than you started? Now this isn't necessarily and unfounded fear; I have witnessed many individuals who have jumped from the frying pan into the fire. Yet, it's not because they attracted failure or they actually made a step that warranted criticism. It's because they started with the wrong belief system that is finite and distorted. If you attempt to shed the armor of trauma to find yourself trapped with no hope for success, it simply means you are coming from a finite perspective, the pseudo-self's deception, and only need to continue taking steps forward until you *rise* to your infinite vision, the Ideal Self's paved path to you becoming whole again.

It's the fear of illness. Will you only come up with a label that is impossible to shed? It is here that you come to learn how defeat and difficulty are regenerative, just as Mother Nature heals her earthly globe. The earth's rooting of new seed; *rejuvenating* from the sun and partnership with our breath, *real-I-zation* that lemonade is made from lemons, hence each blade of grass is necessary for the lawn to spread through the park; *renewing* from the blackened and barren landscape to lush emerald green of paradise; *reviving* to a forest grander than before; *restoring* and providing a home for all creatures and mankind over and over and over; and, *resurrecting* when mankind can only see the ruin and beyond the finite vision.

It's the fear of death; the shedding of the armor won't be enough. You will still be left behind and want to die. The forest does experience a finite death after the fiery inferno destroys everything in its path, and it regenerates to a more beautiful landscape that was previously imagined.

It's the fear of old age, where it's too late – you are what you are, and change is too late in coming. Buying into the adage that "you cannot teach an old dog new tricks." I love the New Age saying, today's thirty is yesterday's forty! Again, age is finite, as we are willing to stand and *rise*, we come to know that *rebounding* is all part of the game.My philosophy is, life is always right and time is an illusion. Hence, you are showing up ath the perfect asge to begin to move past barriers now and break through the cocoon to fly is perfection! Embrace what is!

It's the fear of a *loss of someone* – no doubt you picked this book to read because you have some fear of losing your husband; part of you has bought into your pseudo-self's lie that you are not lovable because you are damaged goods from your PTSD. The goal here is to heal your trauma and heal your marriage. As we know, selfishness of another is something you have no control over, and you may face a time your partner refuses to show up in the marriage. He may make different choices and still place the blame on you. As you root, rebound, and *rise*, and see from your Ideal Self's eyes, you will know that a dissolvement of your marriage does not equate to your failure. In fact, it may open your way to the healing that an unwilling partner's influence will sabotage. You can know that as you stay on the path and work the 7 Steps without detour the infinite wisdom will be available for you to witness the healing process and know the why, what, where, when, and how of where you land. Your purpose will be clear, and you will be on your path completely untethered by any residual from your past pain.

Again, as you *rise* to your greatest heights, you will come to know that all these fears are an illusion. Marcia Grad's parable of *The Princess Who Believed in Fairy Tales* takes the princess on a journey where she discovers that by persevering through her fears you will *rise*. The princess finds herself in the ocean, and she cannot swim. At the moment, she fears she is on the verge of death; she recognizes her dilemma of resigning and allowing herself to sink to the bottom of the oceans or keep wrestling for her life and calling for assistance. As she chooses the latter, a dolphin appears and carries her to shore. She rescued herself by making the decision for fight with all her might, mind, and strength, determined to be undeterred and then came the rescue from the dolphin. It was after the test of the trial that she was reminded she could rise to the occasion and get to her destination.

Robert Forest also wrote a parable called *The Knight in Rusty Armor*, where a knight is infamous for conquering the most ferocious and biggest fire breathing dragons in the land. Yet when he was faced with the need to fight the most monstrous one of all without his shield or his armor, he was also faced with his greatest fear as he no longer had the protection of what he knows from his finite intellect and skills. His survival was dependent upon him standing tall rooted in where he was at in the moment, rebounding from the performance behind the costume and tomb of his rusted armor and *rising* to face his fear by willingly stepping forward to mastering the greatest feat of all this for him. He was prepared; he had the skills and the wisdom to face this fear and conquer the dragon. He remembered the fear of his past belief that he would *burn up* without his armor and knew this was the deceptive limit taught to him by his pseudo-self. Now with the rusted armor shed, his Ideal Self showed up and used the infinite wisdom and skills from infinite resources at his disposal, and he courageously walked through his fear and conquered his enemy.

The training for the princess and the knight had already happened. Just as a butterfly within the cocoon trains for her flight by strengthening her wings, she does not know she can fly until she breaks through the cocoon that has nurtured her and protected her from outside elements. By relying on their faith and persevering work, they evolved to their destinations. Each of the stories end with them both reckoning with the next step ahead of them of reuniting with the mate. They were ready and free to return to their partner in their *resurrected* stated and take the quantum leap to re-creating their dream come true re-union to living happily ever after.

As the journey is complex, growing is continuous, whether conscious or unconsciously driven, and each new experience brings forth the law of opposition in all things with it.

So, again, knowing yourself and where you start is the stronghold for managing the new potential obstacles that comes along the way. Another obstacle that may come your way, is being triggered from your past. This trigger may be in the form of a PTSD memory; a push back and resistance from your spouse or a longing for the familiar – despite it being everything contrary to what is desired.

In his book *Betrayal Bonds*, author Patrick Carnes identifies nine possible trauma states that can predominantly impact you and your marriage as you combat your PTSD.

They are:

1. Trauma reaction occurs when you experience a trigger that creates an emotional reaction greater the present event warrants due to unresolved trauma experience.

2. Trauma arousal is a search for a *pop* or emotional spike from presence of danger, violence, risk, and shame to feelings from what is known in the past.

3. Trauma pleasure is the attraction and urge for pleasurable stimulation from the extreme danger, violence, risk, or shame.

4. Trauma blocking is the numbing, blocking, and overwhelming residual effects from the trauma events.

5. Trauma splitting occurs when one is unable to integrate the effects of trauma, causing a splitting in their personality and reactions.
6. Trauma abstinence is a pattern of compulsive deprivation and self-sabotage by shame or anxiety.
7. Trauma shame is a development of lack of self-worth and self-loathing from the traumatic experience.
8. Trauma repetition occurs as repeating behaviors occurring or sought after, re-creating the trauma cycle.
9. Trauma bonds is another word for *woundology*, attachments occurring in the presence of danger, shame, or exploitation.

Finding yourself trapped in any one of these states manifests in the following behaviors and/or experiences:

Flashbacks; intrusive thoughts; insomnia; triggered associations; troubling dreams; physical symptoms; hyper vigilance; living in extremes; bipolar cycles; and coping mechanisms of overwhelm to the extent of not being able to function.

As you now know this does not have to be *who* you are, these ramifications can all be left in the past as you break out of your rusted armor, cocooning with your inner healer and flying in unison in wing together with the husband of your dreams. I love the lesson I learned from my yoga training, that true change comes from intention, effort, and consistent practice. So, I challenge you to adopt this philosophy as you commit to your *Triangle of Mastery's 7 Steps of Root, Rebound, and Rise* being the lifetime blueprint for navigating forward to staying above and beyond the ceiling of the finite. And remember the empowered insight of living your Ideal Self's dream with the conviction to *be* your purpose.

Ironically, the familiarity of the past creates another illusion of comfort in that it's *what you know* versus the evolvement of becoming who you are. By living in the *now*, you are also contracting with the unknown, and the pseudo-self associates the unknown with fear. Knowing that as you *rise* and refine your vision, your Ideal Self's insight overrides the shortsightedness of your past pseudo-self and a new comfort of love and service in your new heart's desire emerges. The newfound freedom to fly off to new adventures fills your being with the marvelous and wonderous beginnings of a life vision toward the infinity, where continuously growth and wholeness is yours.

Taking the leap to fly requires crossing a transformational bridge which is into unknown territory for the butterfly. Freeing herself from the cocoon is the only way for the opening to take hold of the unknown and test her wings to fly. Her teacher, as for all of us, is her inner whisperings from her Ideal Self. As she learned during her tutoring within her cocooning, she could rebound by rooting to *rising* and she evolved through the *7 Steps* of her *Triangle of Mastery*. The inner knowing, present as she exited the cocoon, readies her for flying being the natural option for *rising* in her journey. The *rise* of the butterfly is reminiscent to reaching the doorway between your immortal soul and your earth-bound personality to becoming your Ideal Self.

At this point, you have done the pre-requisite self-work – through each of the 7 Steps that brought you to this point – you can *now* talk to your inner healer and ask the questions you most want answered. Your Ideal Self can give you access to your Book of Life or Akashic records which contain your true-life purpose and remind you that you are a perfect being made of love and light. Your story includes the happy ending of the discord in your marriage that will lead you to getting a grip of your PTSD. The full story unfolds as you open your Star Chakra and *rise*, stepping through the veil that separates your earthly story from your eternal purpose. Entering the place where there is no time and no space offers the gift of being present to see you as your spouse sees, hear as he hears, and know as he knows, and then together discard the residue of the gross matter that bounds you to the past and keeps you from replaying a lifetime theme and patterns of wear and tear, which keep you chained to your trauma and fractured your union.

Rising, as symbolized by the eighth Chakra, is the gate that leads to the Divine and known as *Wiracocha*, or source of the sacred. It's the Chakra that holds the story that is now needed or desired in the expansion of your love story. You can now rid your life of all residual energy by clearing out once and for all the past debris as you, being your Ideal Self, open the Book of Life's story that all relationships are a sacred commitment between you, your spouse and God. This triangle of unison represents the purpose *To Love… & Beyond*, as depicted in the symbolic signature of *The Triangle of Mastery*. As the three-way union reaches up with a broken heart and contrite spirt to be greeted with the outreached hand of the third partner, your Creator holds the key to the Book of Life where the answers to the why, what, when, where, and how lie. Actively engaging on this enlightened unity, you shed all patterns that keep you from unconditionally loving your spouse and receiving his love for you. The answers to full healing of any remains of the broken heartedness will be found while forever expanding to a full heart and joining the yin and yang connectedness for one complete eternal circle of living a life from the inside out.

Together, you and your husband's vibrations raise the marriage to a new paradigm, drawing you to a new community of like-minded people, who have *risen* and join you as masterminds moving toward greater heights and infinite possibilities.

Already having raised your awareness of being intuitive, *rising* and showing up as your Ideal Self, your powers of intuition will increase, as well as other latent talents that will reveal themselves as you continue vibrating and building new capabilities that your Ideal Self bestows on you. As you *rise*, you are also engaging your eternal nature. You are doing this by not just seeking to learn your earthly roles; you are also following personal inspiration and revelation where fear cannot reside. You are literally swimming within the realm of unquenchable love and joy.

Your record of your soul's contract or life purpose will manifest and be seen by you. You can image the empowerment at your reach by reading the earthly contract with which you entered this world and the lessons attached that you chose to learn and evolve. Your soul's purpose is always clear to your Ideal Self and the possibilities are endless.

As you *rise* and see from the horizon, like the butterfly – your energy is activated and open, allowing a shift to your focus. As your Ideal Self is kept in the forefront, your vision will guide you to work so your soul's sacred commitment to a three-way contract to live a happy union comes true.

As you *rise*, your fears are extinguished with the knowledge that your contracts are sacred, and the marriage is the fertile ground for your love to blossom accordingly. In turn, your growth continues; you become more spiritually compassionate toward all, especially your spouse, and come to know that he is part of the same journey. Each of you play your own and jointly important roles in the interconnected reunion to which you commit and of which you desire to be a part.

By *rising* up, you can now peek at that huge spiritual tapestry, experience true unity, which is followed by unconditional love for one another and from the Divine. Once you both feel the divine power of your mutual love, you both can reflect that love in your actions and let it spread like ripples in a pond. Imagine what the world could be like if everyone had golden halos from their open Star Chakra, beaming love and compassion onto their marriages.

Now part of the healing strategy entails bringing your full self to the relationship. We are all human and our strengths and weaknesses make us up. By bringing all of you to the forefront, your Ideal Self fuses her subtle being into your battered being, clears out the past trauma, and patterns and accelerates the healing process and spiritual illumination.

Then by adding affirmations as the frosting on the cake toward mitigating any second wind fears any last barriers are broken, you can *rise* and refine the *you* that you desire to be.

Affirmations are positive *I am* statements that evolve into beliefs and represent your truth as manifested into your being. The following are examples of affirmations:

I am feeling, thinking, and lovingly expressing my vision of divine purpose now.

I am one with my husband as we are lovingly bound.

I am living the life where all my dreams come true.

I am living the truth and purpose I desire to manifest.

As you can now see, fear is the delusion. You truly have nothing to fear but fear itself. So I challenge you to take action now. You are not alone. You are an energy being who has the formula and the presence of *now* to work with. I hope you walk the walk of *The Triangle of Mastery's 7 Steps of Root, Rebound, and Rise* and come to be your Ideal Self and show up as the Princess to your Prince Charming to live happily ever after. To see a color illustration of *The Triangle of Mastery's Step "To Love...& BeYond": Rise,* download the free companion PDF to this book at aplace2turn.com.

Chapter Thirteen:

Free to Be and Love Happily Ever After

"Our deepest fear is not that we are weak. Our deepest fear is that we are powerful beyond measure. It is our light, not our darkness that most frightens us. We ask ourselves, who am I to be brilliant, gorgeous, talented, fabulous? Actually, who are you not to be? You are a child of God. Your playing small does not serve the world... As we are liberated from our own fear, our presence automatically liberates others."
— Nelson Mandela

N ow that you have the keys to becoming your Ideal Self and making your dream marriage come true and living happily ever after, I am confident that you too will achieve your evolution with *The Triangle of Mastery's 7 Steps to Root, Rebound, Rise* to be whole, live with joy, and re-ignite the passion in your marriage. The result of being free is *love*. Love is the healing balm from within in its unquenchable abundance and safely preserved by your Ideal Self. As life happened and sent you on detours that challenged your fairy tale endings read about in books as a child, your evolution diverted to the outside in from the inside out. The fallout is the lost sight of your Ideal Self, and this is the feeding ground for PTSD, developmentally and environmentally. As you gain the tools and insight to *rise* above the distortions of life happening to you and make the choice to allow life to happen for you, you can find your way back, re-engage, and evolve emotionally, mentally, physically, socially, and spiritually in maturation and consciousness learning to love yourself and your spouse.

From our tribe, we are conditioned on how to begin our journey for this earthly trek. This begins before we have any power of choice in developing our individual ways of winning in life via creating strategies for *reviving* and *resurrecting* within the family unit. So, it is of no surprise that your strengths and paradigms for shaping and forming yourself are some of the same traits gained with the tribal upbringing. In fact, so ingrained these traits show up unconsciously as you seek to secure love and approval, especially within your marriage. They are also the coping mechanisms you fall back to when confronted with challenges that come in your present life. These traits form your ego. Your ego is your personality, identity, and beliefs formed during those imprinting years, especially zero to seven years old. This is a good thing, as we need an ego. It is our ego that we use to interact with others and function within our reality. Yet, our ego is in fact our *little* brain, as its function is to serve our biology. It seeks to keep you safe and *in the know* by working as a reducing valve to filter, to maintain status quo, and to play safe. As a child before we launch on our own path, this serves us well. As an adult when we need to keep our biology safe as real harm (emotionally, mentally, physically or spiritually) is in our life, our ego can be our friend. Yet when you hide behind your ego, you then fall out of your world of creative imagination, the habit of daydreaming something different, and lose the opportunity to *rise* to a life free from your PTSD.

Instead, you are stuck in the chokehold of your past trauma and left with the creation of your *insanity* of a tumultuous marriage. The *insanity* comes from insisting on carrying around your less successful, underused, and misaligned traits gained from your tribe and keep on insisting to make them work for you, as you only know what you know. Yet in doing so, you are anchored down in the throes of defeat and left with the carnage of shame. Your ideal Self becomes blocked by the cloak of shame and leaving you with a shadow of yourself. When this happens, a sense of self is lost and out of the shadows *rises* your pseudo-self. Happiness and healthiness do not come from ego-led agendas, as your pseudo self only has a threat-oriented focus, expecting another battle ahead and seeks to avoid the next hurts. This short and lopsided perspective keeps you on the merry-go-round of horror. This leads to a faulty belief that the ego feeds on, that is you are and will be imperfect and incomplete at our highest and best Self, so why try? Then you add insult to injury by projecting the identical message onto your marriage and this too becomes buried alive and unable to manifest its full expression of love and endless joy. A marriage built on an ego-led agenda is one of conflict and strife where it becomes seemingly impossible to dig yourselves out of the debris. As long as you and then your union identify with images of contention, you will unconsciously defend this stand. These defense mechanisms are ones built from fear and insecurity, rather than love and wholeness. This inauthenticity is the poison that has eroded your hope, faith, and all sight of the core values created as you root, rebound, and *rise*.

The challenge then is to question your desire to explore from the inside out. Take this moment to meditate and contemplate how imminent it is for you to start to show up and live your life. Do you have the stamina and courage to tap into your egoless center where your flow of wisdom resides to carry you forward? Are you ready to make the commitment to enter your state of being to *be*-coming? Are you ready to tap into your greatest interpersonal gift, that is becoming personally vulnerable, working with another to mirror back your progress, even during the hardest of times? If you are, *The Triangle of Mastery's 7 Steps of Root, Rebound, and Rise* is set to get you up and running, safely and assuredly. It's your choice, and with choice comes liberation, and with liberation you are free to *rise* to your highest of state of self-*real-I-zation* and live the fulfillment of having become your Ideal Self.

You use your ego to analyze and make judgment calls in order to learn in life. You are then meant to spring from your ego, shed whatever Shadow you have acquired along the way, mature out of the pseudo-self, and evolve into your Ideal Self. *The Triangle of Mastery* takes on your journey of personal revelation where you gain an enlightened perspective of how marvelous and wonderful you truly are. As you work *the 7 Steps to Root, Rebound, and Rise,* you will witness a change within you, your biology, chemistry, and spiritual makeup that will progress with you. I have clients who have experienced instantaneous feelings and experiences of wellbeing and others who have enjoyed an extended journey of lessons and growth along the way of achieving their desired wholeness. All clients have found the rewards of knowing someone has their back and the invaluable catalyst of mirroring back their evolution each step of the way.

My goal for you is to *re-awaken* to where you came from and stand tall as you *restore* your marriage from the ground up. By taking ownership of your life from your first breath to your first step you can, then come to the *real-I-zation* that you are the *I am* who will rebound from your PTSD and devastation done to your marriage. You have the tools now to *renew* your love and covenants, knowing you are not alone in your journey. As you *revive* your voice of choice your Ideal Self will radiate all that you are and more. The lessons from your PTSD will surface and give you strength and insight to *restore* your marriage as both you and your spouse *resurrect* from the debris of the past and bask in the light and love energy you bring forward, re-igniting your passion and making your dreams come true. Now that you have the tools, you can get to work and success will be yours, and if you desire to *rise* more quickly and succinctly, and with greater clarity you can with me. *I am* on your team. As Napoleon Hill so humbly wrote in his book *Outwitting the Devil*, "Two minds are greater than one." This book journals his thirty-year trek toward getting a grip of his past and his trials and tribulations that he endured by doing it alone. He emphasizes that the gifted key to achieving your heart's desire faster and better is to have a mastermind team. My mentoring package is just that: a mastermind commitment to ensure your success in walking through and mastering each step toward living happily ever after.

Love is a power and an essence that is meant to be shared human being to human being – heart to heart. Achievement in life is better and faster with the pure essence of love, working hand in hand to become a pro-totype for you to recreate the success model with your marriage. Again, we know what we know. There is no learning like experiential hands-on learning. Again, we are beings of energy, as a Hypnotherapist and Quantum Healer, these gifts come with the package. By working with me, I will gift you the healing modalities which intuitively speaks to us that will enhance each step of your progression. There are 7 Steps that equates to seven energy healing sessions, which are meant to solidifying and integrate your new insight and paradigm shifts for setting you free to *be*. This gift is valued at a cost, yet the monetary value pales in the light of the miraculous change that will come from the inside out. Again, I have developed *The Triangle of Mastery's 7 Steps of Root, Rebound, and Rise* to stand alone as a roadmap for your personal evolution and formula for re-igniting the love back into your marriage. If you want to integrate and more deeply and assuredly *rise* of your highest and best Self, my mentoring program will give you mastermind success. If you picked this book up and read through to the end, then seventy-five percent of your success has occurred; I congratulate on this endeavor alone and add my deepest heartfelt gratitude for honoring me with your time, energy, and belief in what I believe to be inspired work from our Master Creator, God Himself. I know your success is waiting for you and as you succeed, you will be a light that will shine the path for all those you touch in life. For this I also express gratitude as we all are impacted by the evolvement of one another. Love begets love. Namaste and Amen.

Acknowledgments

I want to express heartfelt gratitude to my husband Patrick for *always* believing in me. Thank you for being my rock and walking through the trenches and embracing rituals and symbols sacred to us to getting to the other side. Life is truly miraculous!

Thank you to Angela Lauria and The Author Incubator's team, as well as to David Hancock and the Morgan James Publishing team for helping me bring this book to print.

Thank You

Thank you for reading! Download the Free companion PDF to this book at aplace2turn.com providing a visual to refer to as a blueprint mapping your personal evolution through the *7 Steps to Root, Rebound, and Rise.*

I am so excited that you have taken the first step to show up for yourself. I'd love to hear how you are getting a grip of your PTSD and creating your *dream come true* marriage.

Please email me *now* to receive your own *Start Where You Are At Trauma Assessment* that will score your starting place and what beginning steps to take to successfully get a grip *now*. And for sharing back your score, you will receive a personalized blueprint of what is your best step-by-step plan toward breaking free to *be.*

And for the heck of it–after you have completed this milestone and upon confirmation of receiving your blueprint along with a brief share of your experience of reading my book and the follow-through process, I will send a courtesy copy of *In The Meantime Guide* for re-igniting the light within you and the passion back in your marriage.

And wait, my thank you doesn't stop here. I am committed to your success. As you work and experience your adventures with your *In The Meantime Guide*, let me know how its working and I will gift you a $500 coupon invitation toward my next *To Love & Beyond Life Mastery Conquest* for only those who have done the work.

I am so excited for your journey as I can envision your success already!

About the Author

D r. Cheri McDonald offers enriched insights to dealing with the intricate challenges of complex trauma as she walks you through the *how to's* of untethering from the ramifications of your PTSD. With the gifted talent of her interweaving her psychotherapy training and her intuitive coaching skills, she guides couples through the shadows of trauma by releasing its destructive grip through imagery, symbols, and rituals and carrying you outside the therapy room *to love and beyond*. Dr. Cheri's teachings open the way to evolve toward complete healing and *resurrecting* your happily ever after marriage and making your dreams come true.

Dr. Cheri's *Triangle of Mastery's 7 Steps to Root, Rebound and Rise* teaches you how to apply these lessons and insights to gain your freedom, renew your purpose, and love once and for all.

Dr. Cheri McDonald is the founder of *A Place to Turn, Inc*. and creator of *To Love...& Beyond*. She helps couples unbury their marriages from the avalanche of PTSD for over 30 years by guiding clients to *resurrecting* themselves first and then bringing their companion up with them.

Dr. Cheri McDonald received her Bachelor of Science at Brigham Young University in Family Sciences in 1983. She continued her education at California Lutheran University where she obtained her Master of Science in Marriage and Family Therapy in 1987, then completed her formal education in 2007 with a Doctorate degree in Philosophy of Clinical Hypnotherapy at Pacific University. Last and most importantly, Dr. Cheri loves people and helps their dreams come true as they break the bands of their complex trauma, then turn around and *resurrect* their marriages from the remaining carnage for a happily ever after life.

Cheri and her husband, Patrick, have raised three sons and a daughter and enjoy their eight grandchildren as they reside in Thousand Oaks, California. Being a wife, mother, and grandmother has been her greatest responsibility and joy in life.

CPSIA information can be obtained
at www.ICGtesting.com
Printed in the USA
JSHW081301050423
39944JS00001B/38

9 781642 797466